Captivate Network is a digital news and entertainment network that has unique access to almost 60 million business professionals monthly through a combination of exclusive video screens inside office elevators and Web site and live events inside building lobbies. Based on several years of viewer feedback and interaction, Captivate's editorial staff has found that its most popular feature is "Word of the Day." Now the company that brings challenging words to some of the most accomplished professionals in North America's premier office towers has put together a fun word-of-the-day book for everyone who wants to improve his or her vocabulary—or just loves learning new words.

# THE
# WORD LOVER'S
# DELIGHT

*Awesome Adjectives,*
*Nifty Nouns, and*
*Vibrant Verbs*
*to Make Your Vocabulary Sizzle*

from the Editors of Captivate.com®

CITADEL PRESS
Kensington Publishing Corp.
www.kensingtonbooks.com

CITADEL PRESS BOOKS are published by

Kensington Publishing Corp.
119 West 40th Street
New York, NY 10018

Copyright © 2009 Captivate Network, a Division of Gannett Satellite
Information Network

All rights reserved. No part of this book may be reproduced in any form or by any means
without the prior written consent of the publisher, excepting brief quotes used in reviews.

All Kensington titles, imprints, and distributed lines are available at special quantity
discounts for bulk purchases for sales promotions, premiums, fund-raising, educational,
or institutional use. Special book excerpts or customized printings can also be created to
fit specific needs. For details, write or phone the office of the Kensington special sales
manager: Kensington Publishing Corp., 119 West 40th Street, New York, NY 10018,
attn: Special Sales Department; phone 1-800-221-2647.

CITADEL PRESS and the Citadel logo are Reg. U.S. Pat. & TM Off.

First printing: July 2009

10 9 8 7 6 5 4 3 2 1

Printed in the United States of America

Library of Congress Control Number: 2009923864

ISBN-13: 978-0-8065-3119-9
ISBN-10: 0-8065-3119-3

*Words are, of course, the most powerful drug used by mankind.*

**—Rudyard Kipling**

# introduction

Welcome to Captivate® Network's *Word Lover's Delight*.

The question you may be asking yourself is, do I really need to know the definitions of words like *extemporize, interdigitate*, or *mythomania*? Will using the word *ephemeral* in an interview help me get a better job? Will I meet the man/woman of my dreams if I know what *snickersnee* means? Will I finally impress my boss if I drop the word *insalubrious* into a conversation?

Well . . .

Think of *The Word Lover's Delight* as a way to spice up your writing, whether it's the great American novel or an inter-office memo. Why use boring everyday words like *disturbance* when you can spice things up by using *kerfuffle* instead? The English language is filled with thousands of imaginative and colorful but little-known words just there for the taking. So even if you're not an aspiring Hemingway or Robert Frost, you'll still have a ball discovering words such as *dolichocephalic, eponym, insouciant, toxophilite, traduce, vituperate*, and *xerophagy*.

A little about us: Captivate.com began as a flash of inspiration during an elevator ride: a video entertainment platform to reach a "captive" audience. Today, it has grown into a leading alternative multimedia company that delivers more than 52 million impressions a month.

One of the most popular features on the network is "Word of the Day." Each of the spotlighted words ranges from moderately difficult to "show-offy." Each word is accompanied by a phonetic pronunciation, its part of speech, a definition, and use in an easy-to-understand sentence.

One last note: Reading *The Word Lover's Delight*, you may be tempted to think we've actually made some of these words up. It's not every day that you come across words like *pachydermatous*. Rest assured, however, that Captivate's team of editors scrutinize every single Word of the Day submission for accuracy and spelling, and to ensure that it really is a member of the English language.

Enjoy.

# THE
# WORD LOVER'S
# DELIGHT

# A

**abasia**

(n.) uh-BEY-zhuh—unable to walk because muscle coordination is impaired

*The governor was seen by the public only in a wheelchair due to abasia.*

**ablation**

(n.) a-BLEY-shuhn—surgical removal of a part of the body

*The fifty-nine-year-old smoker had radio-frequency ablation of her lung cancer tumors.*

**aborning**

(adv.) uh-BOR-ning—while being born

*The young company almost died aborning because of poor management.*

**abrogate**

(v.) AB-roh-gayt—to do away with

*The nation's leader threatened to abrogate the border agreement with the neighboring country.*

**abscission**

(n.) ab-SIZH-un—the cutting off of something

*The barber performed an abscission on Jim's unsightly ponytail.*

**absquatulate**

(v.) ab-SQUAT-u-late—to leave quickly

*The thunderstorm spooked the horse to break the fence and absquatulate.*

**abstemious**

(adj.) ab-STEE-mi-ous—eating in moderation or with restraint

*Jane's abstemious diet at a lunch meeting annoyed her co-workers.*

> Education is the best provision for old age.
>
> **—Aristotle**

**abstruse**

(adj.) ab-STROOS—hard to comprehend

*He was confounded by the abstruse tax documents.*

**abulia**

(n.) uh-BOO-lee-uh—inability to make decisions

*The first symptom of the CEO's mental breakdown was his abulia at the workplace.*

**accumbent**

(adj.) uh-KUM-bunt—reclining

*The accumbent flowers overflowed from the pot while taking in the sun.*

**acerbic**

(adj.) ah-SUR-bik—harsh in tone

*Alan's acerbic comments made Corrin cry.*

**achromatopsia**

(n.) ah-kroh-muh-TOP-see-uh—color blindness

*People with achromatopsia can only perceive black, white, and shades of gray.*

**acouasm**

(n.) ah-KOO-az-uhm—ringing in the ears

*Art had severe acouasm the day after the concert.*

**addle**

(v.) AD-l—to confuse, befuddle

*Too much eggnog addled her thinking.*

**adoxography**

(n.) ah-DOKS-O-gruh-fee—good writing about a trivial topic

*Adam, a master of adoxography, writes in his blog on a daily basis.*

**adscititious**

(adj.) ad-si-TISH-uhs—not inherent; coming from an outside source

*After studying abroad for a year, Alan brought home new, adscititious behaviors.*

**adumbrate**

(v.) a-DUHM-breyt—to vaguely foreshadow

*The entire future of the company was adumbrated in the report.*

**afflatus**

(n.) ah-FLAY-tuhs—divine inspiration; supernatural suggestion

*The writer said the idea for his latest novel was one that originated from spiritual afflatus.*

**agelast**

(n.) AJ-uh-last—a person who doesn't laugh

*Her boss was such an agelast that trying to joke with him was a lost cause.*

**ageusia**

(n.) ah-GYOO-zee-uh—inability to taste

*Cigarette smoking may cause ageusia.*

> I had a terrible education. I attended a school
> for emotionally disturbed teachers.
>
> **—Woody Allen**

**aglet**

(n.) AG-lit—plastic on the end of a lace

*The cracked aglet made the shoelace useless.*

**agrestic**

(adj.) ah-GRES-tik—rustic

*The farmer's agrestic behavior did not mesh well with that of his sophisticated in-laws.*

**ague**

(n.) EY-gyoo—a chill

*The mound of blankets did nothing to relieve Mabel's ague.*

**ailurophile**

(n.) eye-LOOR-oh-fyle—a cat lover

*The ailurophile had a picture of her cat, Cleo, on her desk.*

**akimbo**

(adj.) ah-KIM-boh—set in a bent position

*In the high winds, Miss America's hair was blown akimbo.*

**albescent**

(adj.) al-BES-unt—turning white

*Ellen's albescent face resulted from her learning about the bad news.*

**albumen**

(n.) al-BYOO-muhn—egg white

*Greg doesn't like yolks, so he orders his omelet with just the albumens.*

**aleatory**

(adj.) AY-lee-ah-tor-ee—reliant on luck

*Harold took part in the aleatory game because he enjoyed taking risks.*

**algid**

(adj.) AL-jid—chilly

*The algid man's skin looked to be very clammy.*

**amanuensis**

(n.) ah-man-yoo-en-sis—someone who takes dictation

*Chrissy was the CEO's indispensable amanuensis.*

**amative**

(adj.) AM-uh-tiv—relating to love

*Her amative suggestions were not always welcome in the office.*

**ambit**

(n.) AM-bit—range of influence

*The ambit of the U.S. Federal Reserve extends far beyond the United States.*

**ambrosial**

(adj.) am-BROH-zhul—having a sweet scent or taste
*Walter loved to walk in the park and smell the ambrosial flowers.*

**amusia**

(n.) ah-MYOO-zee-uh—the inability to detect musical tones
*For most amusia sufferers, listening to music is pointless and even unpleasant.*

**anathematize**

(v.) ah-NATH-uh-mah-tahyz—to curse
*Hester Prynne, in* The Scarlet Letter, *was anathematized by society because of her adultery.*

**anatine**

(adj.) AN-uh-tyn—relating to ducks
*The anatine entourage scurried along the shore to join the lone duck in the water.*

**anfractuous**

(adj.) an-FRAK-tchoo-us—snaky; full of twists
*The car handled well on the anfractuous mountain road.*

**animadversion**

(n.) an-ih-mad-VUR-zhun—harsh criticism
*Patrick was the type of guy that would cry from any sort of animadversion from his boss.*

**anomie**

(n.) AN-oh-mee—isolation due to a lack of social control
*Sam, who suffers from extreme anomie, never leaves his house.*

**anosmia**

(n.) an-OZ-mee-uh—inability to smell
*Dave developed a temporary anosmia as a result of his stuffy nose.*

**antediluvian**

(adj.) an-tih-duh-LOO-vee-uhn—ancient

*My co-worker's style is so out-of-date her outfits seem to be antediluvian.*

**anuptaphobia**

(n.) ah-nup-ta-FOH-bee-ah—fear of being alone

*His anuptaphobia drove him to sign up for the online dating service.*

**aphotic**

(adj.) ah-FO-tik—dark

*The diver's dream was to reach the aphotic depths of the sea.*

> Words are, of course, the most powerful drug used by mankind.
>
> —**Rudyard Kipling**

**apiary**

(n.) EY-pee-er-ee—where bees are housed

*Beverly donned a protective bee suit before she entered the apiary.*

**aplomb**

(n.) ah-PLOM—self-confidence

*Most singers on* American Idol *perform with the aplomb of a seasoned veteran.*

**apogee**

(n.) AP-oh-jee—the culmination

*At its apogee, the Mayan civilization made discoveries in agriculture, astronomy, and writing technologies.*

**apoplectic**

(adj.) ap-uh-PLEK-tik—very angry

*He was so apoplectic his face was purple with rage.*

**arcanum**

(n.) ar-KEY-nuhm—a secret

*The linguist could not get through the arcanum of computer programming languages.*

**arrears**

(n.) ah-REERZ—late in fulfilling payment or promise

*Rod's account was in arrears with the mafia, so the mobster was forced to send his men to collect.*

**arriviste**

(n.) ah-ree-VEEST—one who recently acquired high position but not respect.

*The arriviste tried fruitlessly to be accepted into society.*

**arrogate**

(v.) AR-uh-geyt—to claim without right

*My dog arrogates my bed every night before I go to bed.*

**aspersion**

(n.) ah-SPUR-zhuhn—slander

*I try to ignore aspersions cast upon politicians and celebrities.*

**assiduity**

(n.) as-ih-DOO-ih-tee—diligent effort

*The employees performed their duties with the same assiduity as their managers.*

**ataraxia**

(n.) at-uh-RAK-see-uh—peace of mind

*Abby left her BlackBerry at home so that she could achieve absolute ataraxia on vacation.*

**atelier**

(n.) at-l-YAY—workshop

*The garage served as the painter's atelier.*

**atrabilious**

(adj.) at-ruh-BIL-yuhs—morbid, gloomy

*The atrabilious man was in no mood for jokes.*

**attar**

(n.) AT-ahr—a perfumed oil derived from flowers

*The rare attar sold for hundreds of dollars.*

**aubade**

(n.) oh-BAHD—a song greeting the dawn

*As Elaine watched the sunrise, she heard the birds singing their aubade.*

**augur**

(v.) AW-ger—bode

*The broken alarm clock and burnt coffee did not augur well for Marvin's first day of work.*

**august**

(adj.) aw-GUHST—awe inspiring

*The august words of Helen's professor led her to pursue a career in education.*

**austral**

(adj.) AW-strul—of or coming from the southern hemisphere

*Greg was an austral man through and through, from his taste in food to his accent.*

**autochthonous**

(adj.) aw-TOK-thuh-nuhs—native

*Hank felt like an outcast when he moved to Africa and was surrounded by autochthonous people.*

**autodidact**

(n.) aw-toh-DAHY-dakt—a person who is self-taught

*An autodidact by nature, Amy taught herself German before her trip to Vienna.*

**avuncular**

(adj.) ah-VUHNG-kyuh-ler—friendly, like an uncle

*Tom's older co-worker showed an avuncular concern for his well-being.*

# B

**badinage**

(n.) bad-n-AZH—banter

*Zoe invited friends over for an evening of badinage over a bottle—or two—of pinot.*

**bailiwick**

(n.) BAY-lih-wik—a person's talent

*The professor's bailiwick is mathematics.*

**baksheesh**

(n.) BAK-sheesh—a tip for service

*The foreigner paid baksheesh to the customs official.*

**banausic**

(adj.) buh-NAW-zik—dull, routine

*After years of banausic assembly-line work, Shawn found an exciting job at a media company.*

**barbate**

(adj.) BAHR-beyt—bearded

*Once meticulously clean-shaven, he was now barbate.*

**barratry**

(n.) BAR-uh-tree—groundless, persistent lawsuits

*Attorneys involved in barratry may be suspended from the practice of law or disbarred.*

> Abuse of words has been the great
> instrument of sophistry and chicanery, of
> party, faction, and division of society.
>
> —John Adams

**beatitude**

(n.) be-AT-i-tud—extreme joy
*Henry woke up in a state of beatitude on Friday.*

**becalm**

(v.) bi-KAHM—to deprive of wind
*The schooner was becalmed in the middle of the ocean,
surrounded by the setting sun.*

**bedizen**

(v.) bih-DY-zuhn—to dress gaudily
*The gem-bedizened woman was sparkling from head to toe.*

**bellicose**

(adj.) BEL-ih-kohss—favoring battle
*The country had a history of bellicose tendencies.*

**bemire**

(v.) bee-MAYUHR—cover with mud
*The soldiers bemired themselves as a camouflage.*

**bibliophage**

(n.) BIB-lee-uh-feyj—a bookworm
*Barry the bibliophage likes to spend his Friday nights at the
library.*

**bibulous**

(adj.) BIB-yu-luhs—fond of drinking alcohol

*The harsh daylight was unkind to the old man's grizzled, bibulous face.*

**biddable**

(adj.) BID-uh-bul—obedient

*The biddable assistant never once argued with his boss.*

**billet**

(n.) BIL-it—a job

*Debbie decided to take a billet that she did not necessarily enjoy but that paid well.*

**billingsgate**

(n.) BIL-ingz-gayt—vulgar language

*Kathy's never-ending stream of billingsgate made everyone at the dinner party cringe.*

**bissextile**

(adj.) by-SEKS-tayl—leap year

*George was born in a bissextile year and has a birthday only every four years.*

**blandishment**

(n.) BLAN-dish-ment—flattery

*She ignored the salesperson's blandishments.*

> Words are a lens to focus one's mind.
>
> —**Ayn Rand**

**blatherskite**

(n.) BLATH-er-skayt—a babbling fool

*The meeting ran long and nothing got accomplished because it was run by a blatherskite.*

**blimpish**

(adj.) BLIM-pish—pompous, windbaglike

*The waiter was fed up with the restaurant's blimpish clientele.*

**bloviate**

(v.) BLOH-vee-eyht—to communicate in a pompous way

*At his high school reunion, the Yale graduate bloviated about his academic standing.*

**bombinate**

(v.) BOM-buh-neyt—to buzz

*The computers bombinate if they are left on for too long.*

**boodle**

(n.) BOOD-l—a bribe

*The woman gave her secretary a boodle to destroy the files.*

**borborygmi**

(n.) bawr-buh-RIG-mahy—rumbling sounds made by the digestive tract

*Her borborygmi were embarrassingly loud; she needed breakfast now.*

**boscage**

(n.) BOS-kij—a bunch of trees or bushes

*Bill spent the afternoon trying to tame the massive boscage in his backyard.*

**bouleversement**

(n.) bool-VAIR-suh-MAWN—an overtaking
*Digital downloads have caused a bouleversement of music-buying trends.*

**brabble**

(v.) BRAB-uhl—to argue over something petty
*The couple brabbled over which movie to see.*

**bravura**

(n.) brah-VYOOR-ah—a showy display
*The figure skater's bravura made his routine a real crowd-pleaser.*

**bric-a-brac**

(n.) BRIK-uh-brak—sentimental trinkets
*The garage sale featured books, toys, and other bric-a-brac.*

**brinkmanship**

(n.) BRINK-man-ship—pushing a dangerous situation to the limit
*South Korea accused North Korea of brinkmanship.*

**brio**

(n.) BREE-oh—liveliness; spirit
*The Shakespearean actor was acclaimed for performing each role with brio.*

**bristly**

(adj.) BRIS-lee—easily irritable
*The bristly exchange between the defendant and the judge did not bode well for his case.*

**Brobdingnagian**

(adj.) brob-ding-NAG-ee-uhn—gigantic
*The Brobdingnagian couple was destined to have colossal kids.*

> The basic tool for the manipulation of reality
> is the manipulation of words. If you can
> control the meaning of words, you can control
> the people who must use the words.
>
> —**Philip K. Dick**

**bromidic**
> (adj.) broh-MID-ik—stale, clichéd
> *My wife's bromidic TV shows are easy to sleep through.*

**brumal**
> (adj.) BROO-mal—related to winter
> *With the brumal weather finally gone, they enjoyed a drink on the patio.*

**brume**
> (n.) BROOM—mist; fog
> *Unable to see clearly, Barbara drove slowly through the early morning brume.*

**brutalist**
> (n.) BROO-tal-ist—plain, sturdy architecture
> *The dreary skyline was dominated by brutalist structures.*

**bumptious**
> (adj.) BUMP-shuhs—crudely self-confident
> *Unable to listen to Tom's bumptious conversation, Kia ended the date early.*

**bunkum**

(n.) BUNG-kum—insincere talk

*Tony's argument was quickly dismissed as bunkum.*

**busker**

(n.) BUSK-ur—a street entertainer

*Tracy Chapman was a busker in Boston before she was signed to a record deal.*

# C

**cabal**

(n.) kah-BAL—a small group plotting against a leader
*The cabal of jaded cabinet members conspired to kill the president.*

**cachexia**

(n.) kah-KEK-see-uh—sick emaciation
*Cachexia is often seen in cancer and AIDS patients.*

**cachinnate**

(v.) KAK-uh-neyt—to laugh loudly
*Carrie cachinnated until her sides were sore.*

**cacodaemon**

(n.) kak-uh-DEE-muhn—demon
*I have a hard time ignoring the cacodaemon within me that tempts me with treats and sweets.*

> "When I use a word," Humpty Dumpty said
> in rather a scornful tone, "it means just what
> I choose it to mean—neither more nor less."
>
> **—Lewis Carroll**

**cacoëthes**

(n.) kak-oh-EE-theez—undeniable urge

*Chris developed a cacoëthes for eggnog during Christmas.*

**cacography**

(n.) kak-OG-ruh-fee—bad penmanship

*The computer was the best thing that happened to Jacqui's cacography.*

**cacophony**

(n.) kak-OF-uh-nee—harsh dissonant sound

*The Iowa native was not accustomed to New York City's cacophony of sounds.*

**cadge**

(v.) KAJ—to beg

*Dennis cadged his parents for money after he graduated from college.*

**caducity**

(adj.) ka-DOO-sit-ee—senility

*On his fiftieth birthday, he developed a fear of caducity.*

**caitiff**

(n.) KAY-tif—a rotten person

*The rival politicians tried to portray each other as caitiffs.*

**calaboose**

(n.) kah-le-BOOS—a prison

*Christine was sentenced to two weeks in the calaboose for stealing office supplies.*

**caliginous**

(adj.) kah-LIJ-uh-nus—dark, gloomy

*Beth fell into a caliginous state when she was fired from her job.*

**callithump**

(n.) KAL-uh-thump—a loud, rowdy parade
*The neighborhood kids would bang pans together whenever they put on their springtime callithump.*

**calumniate**

(v.) kah-LUHM-nee-eyt—slander
*My co-worker likes to calumniate anyone who isn't within earshot.*

**calvous**

(adj.) KAL-vuhs—bald
*My calvous father always burns his head in the summer.*

**camarilla**

(n.) kam-uh-RIL-uh—a secret group of advisers
*Whispering in the president's ear, the camarilla had access to power without bearing responsibility for the effects of their advice.*

> A thousand words will not leave so deep an impression as one deed.
>
> **—Henrik Ibsen**

**canard**

(n.) kah-NAHRD—false story or rumor
*The journalists focused upon the politician's canard during the press conference.*

**canorous**

(adj.) kah-NOR-us—mellifluous, musical

*The birds' canorous sounds herald the arrival of spring.*

**capacious**

(adj.) kah-PAY-shuhs—spacious; roomy

*Her capacious purse weighed ten pounds, and she could never find a thing in it.*

**caprice**

(n.) kah-PREES—an abrupt, unpredictable thought or action

*A momentary caprice compelled Ryan to propose to Rochelle during a trip to Paris.*

**captious**

(adj.) KAP-shuhs—given to finding faults

*The captious critic rarely gave a film more than two stars out of five.*

**carapace**

(n.) KAIR-uh-pace—the thick shell on turtles and crabs

*The lobster's carapace turns red in boiling water.*

**careworn**

(adj.) KAR-worn—haggard

*No cream could clear the worry lines off of Joy's careworn face.*

**caritas**

(n.) KAR-ee-tas—love for everyone

*Evelyn's caritas touched many lives before she passed away.*

**cark**

(n.) KARK—a burden

*Maria's life consisted of so many carks and cares that it led her to check into a mental health clinic.*

**catafalque**

(n.) KAT-uh-falk—a coffin platform
*The casket was placed on the decorated catafalque.*

**catamount**

(n.) KAT-uh-mownt—a wild, argumentative person
*He was a real catamount, always ready for a good brawl.*

**cataplexy**

(n.) KAT-uh-plex-ee—a fright-induced paralysis
*She was overcome by cataplexy at the entrance to the haunted house.*

**caterwaul**

(v.) KAT-er-wol—to cry loudly
*The IT engineers caterwauled over who had the fastest computer.*

**celadon**

(adj.) SEL-ah-don—a light gray-green
*Her celadon eyes turn a vibrant emerald when she wears green clothes.*

> It is a damn poor mind indeed which can't think of at least two ways to spell any word.
>
> **—Andrew Jackson**

**celerity**

(n.) suh-LEHR-i-tee—speed
*Brian dreamed of an Internet connection that moved with celerity.*

**cenacle**

(n.) SEN-uh-kuhl—a writers' clique
*The members of the cenacle gained inspiration from one another's work.*

**cento**

(n.) SEN-toh—writing using only quotes from other authors
*The mosiac poem was a cento comprised of lines from T. S. Eliot, Frost, Whitman, and Longfellow.*

**cephalalgia**

(n.) sef-uh-LAL-juh—a headache
*Bobby's cephalalgia was caused by a reaction to the drugs.*

**cerebration**

(n.) ser-uh-BREY-shuhn—thinking
*Philosophers and scholars celebrate cerebration.*

**cerulean**

(adj.) seh-ROO-lee-an—sky blue
*There was a twinkle in her cerulean eyes.*

**chiliad**

(n.) KILL-ee-ad—millennium
*Y2K fears were proven to be unwarranted at the start of the new chiliad.*

**choleric**

(adj.) KOL-er-ik—easily irritable
*The choleric man was red-faced and ready to burst.*

**chrematophobia**

(n.) krey-mah-toh-foh-bia—a fear of money
*Donald Trump does not suffer from chrematophobia.*

**cicerone**

(n.) sis-uh-ROH-nee—a tourists' guide
*Having lived in the city for years, Julia was a natural fit as a cicerone.*

**cineaste**

(n.) SIN-ee-ast—a movie expert
*The cineaste was able to predict most of the Oscar winners.*

**circumambulate**

(v.) sur-kum-am-BYOO-leyt– to walk around the perimeter
*The picketers circumambulated the building all day long.*

**circumbendibus**

(n.) sur-kuhm-BEN-duh-buhs—a circular way
*The taxi driver took the tourist on an expensive circumbendibus to the hotel.*

**circumlocution**

(n.) sur-kuhm-loh-KYOO-shuhn—use of too many words
*The CEO's hourlong circumlocution made many minds wander.*

**claptrap**

(n.) KLAP-trap—insincere words
*Jason's claptrap was a sure sign that he was bored with the topic of discussion.*

**clinquant**

(adj.) KLING-kahnt—glittering with tinsel
*The Christmas tree was clinquant, shimmering in the light of the fireplace.*

**cloy**

(v.) CLOY—to be too rich or filling
*Chocolates were cloying to Martha after she ate a whole box.*

**coimetrophobia**

(n.) coi-met-ro-FOH-bee-uh—fear of cemeteries

*Evelyn had to face her coimetrophobia when her dad died.*

**colloquium**

(n.) kuh-LOH-kwee-um—a meeting on a specific subject

*The company is holding a colloquium on oil exploration.*

**comestible**

(adj.) co-MES-ti-ble—edible

*Mandy decided the bread was no longer comestible after she saw mold on a slice.*

**commination**

(n.) kom-uh-NAY-shuhn—a condemnation

*The book was a biting commination of authority.*

**commingle**

(v.) koh-MING-guhl—to be mixed

*The singer's lyrics commingle happiness and sadness.*

**compendious**

(adj.) kom-PEN-dee-uss—concise and comprehensive

*The tourism board issued a compendious guidebook.*

**comprador**

(n.) kom-pruh-DOR—a middleman

*Ken employed a comprador to deal with his ex-wife.*

**conative**

(adj.) KON-ah-tiv—purposeful

*Heather's conative demeanor led her to one promotion after another.*

**concatenation**

(n.) kon-kat-n-EY-shuhn—a chain of events

*A random concatenation of events led Charles to quit his job and move to South Dakota.*

**concomitant**

(adj.) kun-kom-uh-tahnt—concurrent

*Valerie quit her job without looking into the concomitant effects of her decision.*

**condign**

(adj.) kon-DAYN—fitting, appropriate

*The judge's sentence was severe but condign.*

**confabulate**

(v.) kon-FAH-byoo-leyt—to informally chat

*The staff confabulated in the boardroom before the meeting was called to order.*

**conflagration**

(n.) kon-flah-GREY-shuhn—a big fire

*Connie stood outside in her bathrobe, watching the conflagration devour her home.*

**confrere**

(n.) KON-frair—a close co-worker

*Jack consulted with his confrere before every business decision he made.*

**congeries**

(n.) kon-JEER-ees—a collection or mound

*The casserole was a vile congeries of leftovers.*

**consentient**

(adj.) kuhn-SEN-tchunt—unanimous agreement

*The board was consentient to appointing the new CFO.*

**contrail**

(n.) CON-treyl—water in an aircraft's wake

*The stunt plane's contrail formed the words "marry me."*

**contumelious**

(adj.) kon-too-MEE-lee-uhs—rudely contemptuous

*Her co-worker's contumelious comments humiliated Hazel, who went to the restroom and cried.*

**conurbation**

(n.) kon-er-BEY-shun—a network of urban communities

*Kathryn moved to the bustling conurbation as soon as she graduated.*

**copestone**

(n.) KOHP-stohn—a finishing touch

*The author's final novel was the copestone of his illustrious career.*

**corpulent**

(adj.) KOR-pyuh-luhnt—overweight

*The corpulent man could not walk on his own.*

**correctitude**

(n.) koh-REK-tih-tood—proper conduct

*The parents tried to keep their children's correctitude in check.*

**corrigendum**

(n.) koh-rih-JEN-dum—an error in writing

*The medical editor tried very hard to avoid the need for a corrigendum.*

**coruscant**

(adj.) kuh-RUS-kant—glittering

*The coruscant rocks look like gold.*

**coruscate**

(v.) KAWR-uh-skeyt—to reflect bright light

*Her one-carat diamond solitaire coruscated under the halogen lights of the elevator.*

**cosset**

(v.) KOS-it—to spoil

*Conor was so cosseted by his mother that he didn't know how to do laundry by age thirty-two.*

**coulis**

(n.) KOO-lee—pureed fruit

*The dessert chef prepared a raspberry coulis to drizzle over the cake.*

**coulrophobia**

(n.) kool-ROH-foh-bee-uh—a severe fear of clowns

*Due to Jody's coulrophobia, she was unable to eat at McDonald's.*

**coxcomb**

(n.) KOKS-kohm—a conceited fool

*He's a coxcomb who hogs the bathroom in the morning.*

> Man does not live by words alone, despite the fact that sometimes he has to eat them.
>
> **—Adlai Stevenson**

**cozen**

(v.) KOHZ-uhn—to cheat or defraud

*The unscrupulous psychic cozened Christine out of her life savings.*

**crapehanger**

(n.) KREYP-hang-gur—a melancholy person

*Joe was such a crapehanger that he would read the obituaries before any other section of the paper.*

**craven**

(adj.) KREY-vuhn—cowardly

*The craven dog cowered in the corner when the cat came in the room.*

**crepuscular**

(adj.) kreh-PUHS-kyoo-lar—dimness during twilight

*The crepuscular rays of sunlight shed an orange glow over the hillside*

**cruciverbalist**

(n.) KROO-suh-vur-bah-list—a word enthusiast

*The cruciverbalist had books of crossword puzzles lying around the house.*

**cryptonym**

(n.) KRIP-toh-nim—code name

*Inventor Dean Kamen chose "Ginger" as the cryptonym for his revolutionary transportation device.*

**cucurbitophobia**

(n.) kyoo-kur-bit-o-FOH-bee-uh—fear of pumpkins

*Penelope's naked porch on Halloween was a testament to her cucurbitophobia.*

**cumshaw**

(n.) KUHM-shaw—a tip

*Steven was dumped by his date after he gave their waiter a less than generous cumshaw.*

**cunctation**

(n.) kungk-TEY-shun—procrastination

*Abby's cunctation forced her to stay late at work to finish her assigned projects.*

# D

**daltonism**

    (n.) DAWL-ton-iz-um—unable to see the difference between red and green

    *Stoplights present a challenge to people who suffer from daltonism.*

**debouch**

    (v.) dee-BOWTCH—to exit a small space onto an open ground

    *The crowd cheered as the baseball players debouched onto the field.*

**defalcate**

    (v.) di-FAL-keyt—to misuse funds, embezzle

    *It's hard to believe the minister would defalcate such a large sum of money.*

**defenestrate**

    (v.) dee-FEN-uh-streyt—to toss out a window

    *I defenestrated Mark's clothes to the pavement when we broke up.*

**dégagé**

    (adj.) day-ga-ZHEY—laid back

    *He envied the surfers for their dégagé lifestyle.*

**degust**

    (v.) di-GUHST—to savor

    *I am more fulfilled when I degust my meal instead of devouring it.*

**deipnosophist**

(n.) dayp-NOS-uh-fist—a good conversationalist
*A skilled deipnosophist can turn dinner doldrums into an intellectual feast.*

**delectation**

(n.) dee-lek-TAY-shun—happiness
*Joey's promotion was the cause of his delectation.*

**deleterious**

(adj.) del-uh-TEER-ee-us—destructive
*The nutritionist educated her on the deleterious effects of a poor diet.*

**deliquesce**

(v.) del-lik-WESS—to melt
*They ate their ice cream quickly as it began to deliquesce in the heat.*

**delitescent**

(adj.) del-ih-TES-uhnt—dormant
*Alvin preached against the delitescent evils that live in all of us.*

**démarche**

(n.) day-MARSH—a plan or strategy
*Lionel's mother suggested a tutor as a démarche to help him improve his grades.*

**demit**

(v.) dih-MIT—to give up a position
*Stefanie's co-workers did not want her to demit her position.*

**deracinate**

(v.) dah-RAS-ah-neyt—to uproot
*By arresting the head of the mafia, authorities effectively deracinated the mob.*

**derision**

(n.) di-RIZH-uhn—mockery

*The shoddy report elicited derision from the board members.*

**desideratum**

(n.) dih-sid-uh-REY-tum—something believed to be vital

*Some people do not consider love a desideratum of marriage.*

**desuetude**

(n.) DES-wih-tood—disuse

*The old dilapidated house has long been in a state of desuetude.*

**desultory**

(adj.) DES-ul-tor-ee—random conversation

*His desultory presentation left the audience totally confused.*

> Words—so innocent and powerless as they are, as standing in a dictionary, how potent for good and evil they become, in the hands of one who knows how to combine them!
>
> **—Nathaniel Hawthorne**

**deucedly**

(adv.) DOO-suhd-lee—insanely

*She was deucedly in love with the guy from the mailroom.*

**devoir**

(n.) duv-WAHR—act of honor

*Seth paid his devoirs to his father by leaving flowers at his gravesite every few months.*

**diapason**

(n.) dahy-uh-PEY-zuhn—a burst of harmonious music
*Paul proposed to Ellen as the symphony finished its performance with a booming diapason.*

**diaphanous**

(adj.) dahy-AF-uh-nuhs—delicate, sheer
*She packed away her diaphanous summer wardrobe.*

> All speech, written or spoken, is a dead
> language, until it finds a willing and
> prepared hearer.
>
> —**Robert Louis Stevenson**

**diatribe**

(n.) DAHY-uh-tryb—a harsh attack
*The podium speaker's talk quickly turned into a diatribe against the health-care system.*

**dido**

(n.) DAYH-doh—a prank
*John's teacher said his dido was not funny and he was suspended.*

**digerati**

(n.) dij-uh-RAH-tee—people who know a lot about technology
*Bill Gates and Steve Jobs are members of the digerati.*

**dilatory**

(adj.) DIL-uh-tawr-ee—characterized by procrastination
*His wife disapproved of his dilatory tendencies.*

**dingle**

(n.) DING-guhl—a tiny valley full of trees

*The businessman dreamt of building a small cabin in a remote dingle.*

**disambiguate**

(v.) dis-am-BIG-yu-eyt—to make sense by rephrasing

*He disambiguated his previous statement to avoid misconception.*

**discomfit**

(v.) dis-KUHM-fit—to embarrass

*The obnoxious wedding singer discomfited the guests.*

**discursive**

(adj.) di-SKUR-siv—rambling

*The old friends held a discursive dialogue for hours, catching up and reminiscing.*

**dishabille**

(n.) dis-ah-BEEL—characterized by dressing carelessly

*Casey lounged around in dishabille during the weekend.*

**distrait**

(adj.) dis-TREYT—distracted

*She was distrait all day at work, thinking about her Valentine's date.*

> Speech is the mirror of the soul.
>
> **—Publilius Syrus**

**ditherer**

(n.) DITH-er-er—someone who cannot make a decision

*She is a ditherer when it comes to choosing what to wear.*

**docent**

(n.) DOH-sent—a lecturer or tour guide

*He worked as a docent at the museum on the weekend to make some extra money.*

**doddered**

(adj.) DAW-derd—enfeebled

*The hockey team was doddered after a long playoff game.*

**doggerel**

(adj.) DAW-ger-uhl—a crudely constructed, funny verse

*A silly doggerel ran through Doug's head during the meeting.*

**dolichocephalic**

(adj.) dol-i-koh-suh-FAL-ik—having a long head

*Dan's dolichocephalic head made him resemble a horse.*

**dolor**

(n.) DO-ler—depression

*The constant rain just made his dolor more intense.*

**donnybrook**

(n.) DON-ee-brook—a fight

*Each family dinner seemed to end in a donnybrook.*

**doughty**

(adj.) DOW-tee—fearless, valiant

*The doughty man survived a week in the forest by eating berries.*

**doula**

(n.) DOO-luh—birthing aide

*Renee's doula provided emotional and physical support during the delivery.*

**dovish**

(adj.) DUH-vish—preferring a peaceful solution to a fight

*The dovish child was known for breaking up fights in the playground.*

## draconian

(adj.) drah-KOH-nee-uhn—harsh, severe

*The struggling company was forced to make draconian budget cuts.*

## dragoon

(v.) drah-GOON—to force

*Dennis' parents dragooned him into going back to school.*

## dubiety

(n.) doo-BY-uh-tee—a sense of doubt

*Dubiety engulfed George as he watched Gertrude amble down the aisle toward him.*

## dudgeon

(n.) DUHJ-uhn—an offensive feeling

*Maryann threw her engagement ring at Thomas in high dudgeon after he admitted to cheating.*

## duende

(n.) DWEN-dey—an ability to charm

*After a few drinks, he would turn up his duende to full throttle around women.*

## dullard

(n.) DUHL-erd—a thick-headed person

*She said he was a dullard because his comments were inappropriate.*

## dysania

(n.) diss-AY-nee-ah—having trouble waking up

*"Another severe case of dysania," he thought to himself as he hit the snooze button for the tenth time.*

**dyspeptic**

(adj.) dis-PEP-tik—crabby, pessimistic

*The dyspeptic boss's mood seemed to get worse when workers were happy.*

**dysphemism**

(n.) DIS-fuh-miz-uhm—substitution of a harsh word for a nicer one

*A dysphemism for died is "croaked."*

**dysphoria**

(n.) dis-FAWR-ee-uh—a state of unease

*She was in a state of dysphoria on her first blind date.*

# E

**ebullient**

(adj.) eh-BUHL-yuhnt—chock full of enthusiasm

*The head cheerleader was the most ebullient.*

**éclat**

(n.) ey-KLAH—brilliant show of success

*Adel possessed a passion for stage acting and the éclat that came with it.*

**ecru**

(adj.) EK-roo—light tan, beige

*Once the Christmas tree turned ecru, the family threw it out.*

**ectotherm**

(n.) EK-toh-therm—an animal that cannot heat itself.

*She basks in the sun like a common ectotherm.*

**edacious**

(adj.) i-DEY-shuhs—ravenous

*My edacious tendencies returned during the holiday season.*

**edentulous**

(adj.) ee-DEN-tyoo-luss—toothless

*Greta's rocklike biscuits are not for edentulous people.*

**effete**

(adj.) eh-FEET—decadent, fancy

*He lived an effete life of fast cars, minimalist furniture, and endless martini parties.*

**effloresce**

(v.) ef-luh-RES—to bloom or burst

*The plant's flowers only effloresce every seven years.*

**effluvium**

(n.) i-FLOO-vee-uhm—an invisible vapor

*The rotten vegetables emitted an unpleasant effluvium.*

**eidetic**

(adj.) i-DET-ik—photographic visual imagery

*Maureen was blessed with an eidetic memory.*

**eidolon**

(n.) ahy-DOH-luhn—a ghost

*She dressed up as an eidolon to spook the trick-or-treaters.*

**élan**

(n.) ay-LAHN—enthusiasm

*Emanuel worked with great élan no matter how dull the task.*

**eldritch**

(adj.) EL-drich—strange, eerie

*The darkness crept into the eldritch dungeon.*

**eleemosynary**

(adj.) el-uh-MOS-uh-ner-ee—generous

*The holiday season evokes a spirit of generosity, spurring people
to give to eleemosynary organizations.*

**embonpoint**

(n.) ohn-bohn-PWAN—plumpness

*Her mother's embonpoint was comforting and familiar.*

**emollient**

(adj.) eh-MOL-yuhnt—softening

*The emollient cream worked wonders on Wendy's dry hands.*

> What if everything is an illusion and nothing
> exists? In that case, I definitely overpaid for
> my carpet.
>
> —**Woody Allen**

**emolument**

(n.) i-MOL-yuh-muhnt—payment for work
*The company's great benefits and emoluments enticed Ernie to quit his old job.*

**emotive**

(adj.) ee-MO-tiv—moving, feeling-stirring
*The artist was known for her emotive paintings.*

**emulous**

(adj.) EM-yoo-luss—eager to emulate
*He was emulous of his older brother's success.*

**enceinte**

(adj.) en-SEYNT—pregnant
*Arnold Schwarzenegger played an enceinte man in the movie* Junior.

**encomium**

(n.) en-KOH-mee-um—a formal tribute
*Her boss delivered a stirring encomium at her retirement party.*

**enervate**

(v.) EN-er-vayt—to drain of energy
*She felt enervated after finishing the Olympic marathon.*

**englut**

(v.) en-GLUT—to guzzle
*Darrell englutted a large glass of water after his workout.*

**ensorcell**

(v.) en-SOR-suhl—to bewitch

*Marie tried to ensorcell Tom with a charm spell.*

**entrain**

(v.) en-TRAYN—to be drawn along

*The president was entrained by a flock of reporters.*

**ephemeral**

(adj.) i-FEM-er-ahl—fleeting

*Evan's ephemeral popularity ended in third grade when he cried in the playground.*

**epicene**

(adj.) EP-ih-seen—having feminine qualities

*The epicene statue of Liberace was hailed by visitors as a true representation of the man.*

**epigone**

(n.) EP-i-gohn—a lowly imitator.

*Kirk Douglas is a legend, and his son Michael is no epigone.*

**epistemology**

(n.) eh-piss-tuh-MOL-uh-jee—the study of the source of knowledge

*The philosopher's epistemology concerning modern thought was severely flawed.*

**epizootic**

(adj.) ep-uh-zoh-OT-ik—an epidemic affecting one kind of animal

*The bird flu epizootic scare has spurred some people to stop eating poultry.*

**eponym**

(n.) EP-uh-nim—a person whose name is used for something else
*Amerigo Vespucci, an Italian merchant who explored South America in 1499, is the eponym for "America."*

**equable**

(adj.) EK-wa-bul—(of a person) tranquil, not easily agitated
*The equable IT manager kept smiling in times of crisis.*

**equanimity**

(n.) EK-wah-nim-ih-tee—composure of mind and temperament
*The tough job required someone with equanimity.*

**equipoise**

(n.) EK-wih-poyz—balance
*The guide warned the tourists not to disturb the rain forest's fragile equipoise.*

**equivocate**

(v.) ee-KWIV-ih-keyt—to speak in a deliberately vague manner
*The politician equivocated when asked about the scandal.*

**equivoque**

(n.) EK-wih-vohk—a double-entendre
*The audience groaned as the speaker used another equivoque.*

**ergophobia**

(n.) ER-go-fo-bee-ah—fear of work
*Her ergophobia grew stronger as her boss became more and more demanding.*

**ersatz**

(n.) UR-satz—artificial substitute
*The five-dollar sunglasses that Ryan bought were nothing more than an ersatz of the original.*

**erudition**

(n.) er-yuh-DISH-un—scholarly learning

*Jan's unimpressive presentation did not reflect her erudition of the topic.*

**esculent**

(adj.) ESS-kyu-lent—fit to be eaten

*He was an expert at finding esculent plants in the wild.*

**espial**

(n.) ih-SPY-ul—the act of observing

*The stargazer added a huge window to his house for the sole purpose of espial.*

**esprit de l'escalier**

(n.) ess-PREE duh les-cal-YEY—coming up with a witty comeback too late

*An esprit de l'escalier popped into her head hours after the insult.*

**estaminet**

(n.) eh-stah-mee-NAY—a tiny café

*The neighbors would meet to have coffee at the estaminet down the street.*

**estival**

(adj.) ES-tuh-vul—having to do with the summer

*Swimming in the ocean is one of the many estival things to be done at the beach.*

**esurient**

(adj.) eh-SOOR-ee-uhnt—ravenous, greedy

*The esurient boy shoveled the chocolate cake into his mouth.*

**ethereal**

(adj.) eh-THEER-ee-uhl—dainty and airy

*Evelyn was a soft, ethereal woman with willowy grace.*

**etiolate**

(v.) ee-tee-OH-leyt—to harm a living thing by lack of light

*Patrick's etiolated body continued to deteriorate in prison.*

**evert**

(v.) ee-VERT—turn inside out

*The security guards asked him to evert his pockets.*

**evincing**

(v.) eh-VIN-sing—to verify, demonstrate

*John was evincing his abilities by producing quality reports.*

**excogitate**

(v.) eks-KOJ-ih-teyt– to mull, conceive or formulate

*The managers excogitated a plan to increase profits.*

**excoriate**

(v.) ek-SKAWR-ee-eyt—to show strong objection to

*The candidate excoriated his rival's speech.*

**exculpate**

(v.) EK-skuhl-peyt—to exonerate

*The lawyer won the case and exculpated his client.*

**exigent**

(adj.) EK-si-juhnt—pressing

*William knew he was in trouble when his boss sent him an exigent e-mail.*

**exiguity**

(n.) ek-suh-GYOO-uht-ee—paucity, smallness

*The exiguity of his income forced Dwayne to move in with his parents.*

**exordium**

(n.) ig-ZOR-dee-um—a start or introduction

*Victor's exordium included a long pause between each word for dramatic effect.*

**exoteric**

(adj.) ek-suh-TER-ik—popular, commonplace for the common man

*Stephen Hawking wrote an exoteric book on the frontiers of science.*

**expiate**

(v.) EK-spee-eyt—to make up for

*The burglar tried to expiate his guilt by apologizing to the victim.*

**expurgate**

(v.) EK-sper-geyt—to remove offensive words

*The editor expurgated the books, making them appropriate for children to read.*

> Knowledge comes, but wisdom lingers.
>
> —**Alfred, Lord Tennyson**

**extemporize**

(v.) ehk-STEM-puh-rayz—to ad-lib

*The comedian extemporized a different act every night.*

**extirpate**

(v.) EK-ster-peyt—to eradicate

*Carol hoped the surgery would extirpate her cancer.*

# F

**fabaceous**

(adj.) fah-BEY-shuhs—having to do with a bean
*The meat lover refused to eat anything fabaceous.*

**facinorous**

(adj.) fah-SIN-uhr-uhs—extremely evil
*The facinorous woman in green could have been mistaken for the Wicked Witch of the West.*

**factious**

(adj.) FAK-shuss—given to conflict
*The new leader hoped to bring unity to the factious political party.*

**factitious**

(adj.) fak-TISH-uss—artificial
*Junk food is full of factitious ingredients.*

**factotum**

(n.) fak-TOH-tuhm—a worker who has a range of responsibilities
*During the summer, Jimmy was Mrs. Miller's factotum: he cut her grass, went food shopping, and made dinner.*

**facultative**

(adj.) FAK-uhl-tay-tiv—elective
*She took a few facultative courses while studying for her degree.*

**fainéant**

(adj.) FAY-nay-ahn—dormant, idle
*Molly spent the entire weekend being fainéant.*

**fantasticate**

(v.) fan-TAS-tik-eyt—to make so remarkable that it seems unreal
*The movie fantasticated the true story with wild embellishments.*

**fantod**

(n.) FAN-tawd—a burst of irritability or fidgets
*Val's husband was in a fantod after she forced him to go shoe shopping.*

**fardel**

(n.) FAHR-dl—load, burden
*The lawyer gave her a fardel of papers to sign.*

**farinaceous**

(adj.) far-ah-NEY-shahs—starchy
*Allen lost fifty pounds on the Atkins diet, giving up all his favorite farinaceous foods.*

**farouche**

(adj.) fah-ROOSH—untamed, shy
*The farouche farm dog didn't adapt well to his new city home.*

**farrago**

(n.) fah-RAH-go—a confused jumble
*The author was slammed for the farrago of nonsense in her new book.*

**fatuity**

(n.) fa-TU-i-tee—silliness
*The crowd laughed at the fatuity of the clown's behavior.*

**fatuous**

(adj.) FACH-oo-uhs—senseless, silly

*The teacher told the boy to wipe the fatuous grin off his face.*

> Education is the best provision for old age.
>
> **—Aristotle**

**fealty**

(n.) FEE-uhl-tee—loyalty

*The CEO promoted employees based largely on their fealty to her.*

**feckless**

(adj.) FEK-lis—uncaring, lazy

*The feckless employee was caught sleeping at his desk.*

**fecund**

(adj.) FEE-kuhnd—able to have babies

*The fecund couple had five children in seven years.*

**feral**

(adj.) FER-ul—wild, untamed

*Monica's feral dog tore up the couch.*

**festal**

(adj.) FES-tahl—festival

*The holiday decorations in the office put the employees in a festal mood.*

**festinate**

(v.) FES-tuh-neyt—to speed up

*Frank hired movers to festinate the moving process.*

**fetid**

(adj.) FET-id—smelling bad

*The fisherman took a shower to wash the fetid smell from his skin.*

**fetor**

(n.) FEH-tor—a rancid smell

*The fetor of rotten food permeated the kitchen.*

**fettle**

(n.) FET-l—state, manner of being

*Jane was in fine fettle and ready to make the presentation.*

**fey**

(adj.) FAY—mystical, unnatural

*For the new children's room, the designers wanted to make a fey environment.*

**filch**

(v.) FILTCH—to take something of little value

*John demanded to know who filched his pen.*

**filigree**

(n.) FIL-ih-gree—anything fragile

*The filigree clasp broke as Emily peered over the bow of the boat.*

**fillip**

(n.) FIL-uhp—a stimulating addition

*A sprinkle of toasted spices was just the fillip the sugar cookies needed.*

**flagitious**

(adj.) flah-JISH-uhs—criminally evil

*The protesters rallied against the dictator's flagitious regime.*

**flaneur**

(n.) flah-NUR—an idler who doesn't work, a man-about-town

*Peter could never be a flaneur because he is such a workaholic.*

**fletcher**

(n.) FLETCH-er—an arrow maker

*Frank's dream of becoming a fletcher began when he saw the
Robin Hood movie.*

**flexitarian**

(n.) flex-ih-TAYR-ee-an—a vegetarian who sometimes eats meat

*The flexitarian joined her friends for a steak dinner.*

**floccinaucinihilipilification**

(n.) flahk-si-naw-si-ni-hi-li-pi-li-fi-KEY-shun—the act of
deeming something worthless

*I tend to be a music snob, and I think my friends are tired of
my floccinaucinihilipilification of pop songs.*

**flummery**

(n.) FLUHM-er-ee—an empty compliment

*The judge was frustrated with the level of flummery
demonstrated by the presenters at the lecture.*

**fogram**

(n.) FOH-gruhm—an outdated old fogy

*The new CEO butted heads with several fograms on the board.*

**foofaraw**

(n.) FOO-fah-raw—insignificant fuss

*The play opened and ended with such fanfare and foofaraw.*

**fop**

(n.) FOP—a man who excessively cares about how he looks

*The fop would frequent the bathroom mirror multiple times
during the workday.*

**fossorial**

(adj.) fo-SAWR-ee-uhl—burrowing

*Aardvarks, armadillos, and moles are all fossorial animals.*

## fractious

(adj.) FRAK-shuhs—wild, unruly

*The fractious fraternity was kicked off campus.*

## frangible

(adj.) FRAN-juh-buhl—able to be broken easily

*Henry was able to knock down the frangible door with just one kick.*

## fratricide

(n.) FRA-tri-sayd—killing your brother

*Cleopatra may have committed fratricide so that her son could be the ruler of Egypt.*

## fribble

(n.) FRIB-uhl—a silly person, thing or idea

*Jerry Seinfeld built a comedic empire based on fribbles.*

---

## Pardonnez-moi, monsieur.

**—Marie Antoinette, after stepping on her executioner's foot**

---

## frigorific

(adj.) frig-oh-RIF-ik—turning cold

*It was a hot day, perfect for a frigorific beer.*

## frippery

(n.) FRIP-uh-ree—flashy clothes

*Stacy wore cozy clothes, whereas her sister preferred frippery.*

## frondescent

(adj.) fron-DES-uhnt—leafy

*Frank glared at the frondescent trees in his yard, dreading the fall.*

**froward**

(adj.) FROH-werd—willfully disobedient

*Patty quit her babysitting job because she was tired of dealing with froward children.*

**frowzy**

(adj.) FROU-zee—dirty, rancid, unkempt

*The dress code policy forbids frowzy clothing.*

**fructuous**

(adj.) FRUHK-choo-uhs—fruitful

*Many of Diane's vegetables were grown in the fructuous soil in her backyard.*

**fugacious**

(adj.) fyoo-GAY-shuhs—lasting for a short time

*Fugacious fall days pass all too quickly, only to be replaced by an unrelenting winter.*

**fulgurous**

(adj.) FUHL-gyer-uhs—looking like lightning

*The fulgurous fire devoured the paper in seconds.*

**fuliginous**

(adj.) fyoo-LIJ-uh-nuhs—sooty or murky

*The fuliginous fish tank desperately needed cleaning.*

**fulminate**

(v.) FUL-muh-neyt—to attack verbally

*The candidate fulminated against his opponent's stance on crime.*

**funambulist**

(n.) fyoo-NAM-byuh-list—an acrobat who uses a tightrope

*The funambulist was so confident in his abilities that he refused to perform with a safety net.*

**funereal**

(adj.) fyoo-NIR-ee-ul—solemn, dismal
*The funereal lyrics evoked the singer's sadness.*

**fungible**

(adj.) FUHN-juh-buhl—exchangeable for something similar
*The investor transferred funds into fungible commodities.*

**furfuraceous**

(adj.) fur-fyuh-REY-shus—containing flaky particles
*Her allergy to dust caused a furfuraceous rash on her arms.*

**fustigate**

(v.) FUHS-ti-geyt—to chastise severely
*Critics fustigated the new Nicole Kidman movie.*

> Only thing worse than watching a bad movie
> is being in one.
> —**Elvis Presley**

**futilitarian**

(n.) fyoo-til-ih-TAIR-ee-uhn—one who believes striving is useless
*The futilitarian will never get a promotion.*

# G

**gabble**

(v.) GAB-uhl—to speak quickly or inarticulately

*Eric would gabble whenever he was nervous.*

**gainsay**

(v.) GAYN-say—to refute

*Ben destroyed the tape so there would be no evidence to gainsay his description of the situation.*

**gallimaufry**

(n.) gal-uh-MAW-free—a jumble; mixture

*Gabby cleaned out her fridge and had a gallimaufry of leftovers for dinner.*

**galoot**

(n.) guh-LOOT—an awkward or gawky person

*The galoot often tripped over his own feet.*

> Stop breathing on me, you long-eared galoot!
>
> **—Yosemite Sam to Bugs Bunny**

**galumph**

(v.) gah-LUHMF—to move inelegantly or heftily

*The toddler galumphed around the room on all fours.*

**gam**

(v.) GAM—to have a pleasant chat
*I enjoy gamming it up with Matt about funny misspellings.*

**gamine**

(n.) GAM-een—a female street urchin who looks like a boy
*Her new pixie haircut made her resemble a little gamine.*

**gasconade**

(n.) gas-kuh-NEYD—arrogant talk
*Gary, boosted by a few glasses of wine, drowned out other conversations with his gasconade.*

**gastronome**

(n.) GAS-truh-nohm—expert in high-quality food and drink
*Hosting a holiday party is intimidating because my friends are fastidious gastronomes.*

**gatophobia**

(n.) gat-o-FOH-bee-uh—phobia of cats
*George developed gatophobia after he was attacked by a stray cat as a child.*

> There are two means of refuge from the misery of life—music and cats.
>
> **—Albert Schweitzer**

**gauche**

(adj.) GOHSH—not having social elegance, uncomfortable
*Paula's gauche demeanor completely disappeared after a few drinks.*

**gelid**

(adj.) JEL-id—incredibly chilly

*The gelid air stung Joe's lungs as he trudged through the snow.*

**georgic**

(adj.) JAWR-jik—relating to farming

*The city slicker couldn't hack the georgic lifestyle.*

**gerent**

(n.) JEER-unt—one who leads or directs

*Part of the gerent's job description was to keep the employees happy and focused.*

**gerrymander**

(v.) JEHR-ee-man-der—to maneuver voting margins to one's political benefit

*The politician was convicted of gerrymandering.*

**gewgaw**

(n.) GYOO-gaw—a flashy trinket, a plaything

*She stuffed her children's stockings with gewgaws.*

**glaucous**

(adj.) GLAW-kuss—soft blue-green

*The glaucous Danube river wound its way through Budapest.*

**gloaming**

(n.) GLOH-ming—nightfall, sundown

*The sky was alight with stars during the gloaming.*

**gloze**

(v.) GLOHZ—to diminish or play down

*Ted glozed over the embarrassing part of the home movie.*

**goldbrick**

(v.)GOHLD-brik—to avoid work, or fool around

*The manager warned his employees not to goldbrick during the CEO's visit.*

**gourmand**

(n.) GOOR-mahnd—a person who eats ravenously or a lot
*The gourmand enjoyed the all-you-can-eat buffet.*

**gourmandize**

(v.) GOOR-mahn-dayz—overindulge or eat boastfully
*The family gourmandized with gusto on Thanksgiving.*

**grandiloquent**

(adj.) gran-DIL-uh-kwuhnt—pretentious, arrogant
*Isaac became increasingly annoying to his date because of his
grandiloquent behavior.*

**gravid**

(adj.) GRAV-id—pregnant, expectant
*The gravid girl stayed in school and earned her diploma despite
the hallway stares and whispers.*

**grig**

(n.) GRIG—an energetic, vivid person
*Janet was as merry as a grig during the holiday season.*

**groak**

(v.) GROHK—to gawk at someone eating with the aspiration
of obtaining food
*Louise resented the way Gary groaked at her every time she had
homemade chocolate chip cookies.*

**grok**

(v.) GRAWK—to comprehend intensely
*I love my wife, but sometimes I wonder if I really grok her.*

**gruntle**

(v.) GRUN-tuhl—to make content
*The employees were gruntled by their yearly bonus.*

**guerdon**

(n.) GUR-dn—a prize that was earned

*Judy lost three pounds—the guerdon for faithfully working out all week.*

**gutbucket**

(adj.) GUHT-buh-kit—of jazz, played in a loud, forceful style

*The streets of New Orleans are filled with the sounds of gutbucket jazz*

**gyre**

(n.) JY-r—a loop or ring

*The turbulent waters swirled in gyres around the rocks.*

## haboob

(n.) hah-BOOB—a dense sandstorm that occurs in North Africa, Arabia, and India
*The haboob left a layer of sand on everything in the Sudanese village.*

## hagiography

(n.) hag-ee-OG-ruh-fee—a life history of a saint or respected person
*The hagiography of Mother Teresa was enlightening.*

## hagridden

(adj.) HAG-rid-n—stressed or disturbed by apprehension
*The gambler left the casino feeling hagridden after losing ten thousand dollars in thirty minutes.*

## halcyon

(adj.) HAL-see-uhn—tranquil, silent, serene
*Once their children moved out, Barbara and Bob enjoyed a halcyon life in Maine.*

## hale

(adj.) HEYL—free from sickness; in good physical shape
*Lance's extended stay in the hospital made him a hale man.*

## hamartia

(n.) hah-mahr-TEE-uh—unfortunate fault
*Oedipus the King's hamartia was his ego.*

## hangdog

(adj.) HANG-dog—ashamed

*Bernie fell into a hangdog silence after uttering the expletive at the meeting.*

## harangue

(n.) huh-RANG—a raucous or pretentious dialogue; tirade

*The boss's weekly harangues last about an hour.*

## hardihood

(n.) HAHR-dee-hood—courage, bravery

*Vince's hardihood stemmed from his tough upbringing.*

## hebdomadal

(adj.) heb-DOM-uh-dul—occurring on a weekly basis

*The son received ten dollars for his hebdomadal allowance.*

## hebetude

(n.) HEB-i-tood—mental exhaustion or stupor

*Jeff's hebetude left him unable to do anything but play computer games.*

## hector

(n.) HEK-tor—a tormenter

*The hector would intimidate his classmates out of their lunch money.*

## helve

(n.) HELV—the grip of a utensil or tool

*The helve of the hammer broke off while Jim tried to remove nails from the wall.*

## henotic

(adj.) hee-NAW-tik—encouraging calm or serenity

*Both sides praised the mediator's henotic handling of their dispute.*

**heterodox**

(adj.) HET-uh-roh-doks—different from some recognized norm or standard; unconventional

*George was openly scorned for his heterodox opinions.*

**hew**

(v.) HYOO—to hack or slice with an ax

*Instead of buying a Christmas tree, he went to the woods to hew a tree.*

**hiemal**

(adj.) HY-eh-mul—associating with winter

*Shoveling the driveway is one of the many hiemal things to be done around the house.*

**highfalutin**

(adj.) hi-fa-LOOT-n—self-important, ostentatious

*Dan left the party, saying he did not like the highfalutin guests.*

**hireling**

(n.) HY-er-ling—a person who works solely for monetary return

*The hireling hated her job but loved payday.*

**hirple**

(v.) HURP-l—to walk with difficulty

*Gary hirpled for a week after working out at the gym.*

**hirsute**

(adj.) HUR-soot—covered with hair

*His hirsute dog left fur all over the sofa.*

**hobbledehoy**

(n.) HOB-uhl-dee-hoy—ill at ease, clumsy young fellow

*After years of traveling, the hobbledehoy matured into a secure man.*

## hoi polloi

(n.) HOI-puh-LOI—ordinary or common folk

*The exclusive club was known for turning away hoi polloi who didn't pass muster.*

## hokum

(n.) HOH-kuhm—stale emotion, gibberish

*He expressed nothing but hokum when meeting his ex-wife's new husband.*

## homichlophobia

(n.) hom-ik-LO-fo-bee-ah—phobia of fog

*She was gripped by a sudden homichlophobia as the fog rolled in.*

## huffish

(adj.) HUFF-ish—conceited, grouchy

*The huffish actor refused to sign any autographs.*

## humoresque

(n.) hyoo-muh-RESK—a quick, cheerful section of music

*The pianist livened up the party with a humoresque.*

## hygrophobia

(n.) hy-gro-FO-bee-ah—phobia of wetness

*Avoid the rain forest in wet season if you suffer from hygrophobia.*

## hymeneal

(adj.) hy-muh-NEE-ul—involving nuptials

*Breaking a glass is a hymeneal tradition of Jewish people.*

**hypnopompic**

(adj.) hip-no-POM-pik—relating to the condition between sleeping and waking

*Luke saw hundreds of spiders crawling on the floor during a hypnopompic hallucination.*

**hypocorism**

(n.) hay-POK-uh-riz-uhm—a pet name

*Gary's hypocorism for his wife, Katheryn, is Kitty.*

# I

**ignoble**

(adj.) ig-NOH-bul—of low ranking; inferior
*Nathan quit his ill-paid and ignoble job to go back to school.*

**ignominious**

(adj.) ig-no-MIN-ee-uss—warranting disgrace or dishonor
*The company was known for its ignominious nepotism.*

**illeist**

(n.) il-EE-ist—a person who uses third person in referring to him- or herself
*"Karl wants a cookie," said the illeist child to his mother.*

**imbroglio**

(n.) im-BROHL-yoh—an intricate misinterpretation or disagreement
*The travelers found themselves in the midst of another imbroglio.*

**imbrute**

(v.) im-BROOT—to descend to the level of a brute
*The* Survivor *contestants became more imbruted every day.*

**immane**

(adj.) ih-MEYN—enormous in character, ferocious
*Attila the Hun's immane presence struck fear into Barbarians and Romans alike.*

**immolate**

(v.) IM-oh-leyt—to kill sacrificially, as by burning
*Erin saw no reason to immolate herself—it was an honest error.*

**immure**

(v.) ih-MYOOR—to confine within walls, imprison
*The detainees were immured in a makeshift prison.*

**immutable**

(adj.) im-YOO-tah-bul—immune to variation
*The scientist believed in the immutable laws of physics.*

**impecunious**

(adj.) im-pih-KYOO-nee-uss—lacking money; poor
*He was impecunious until payday.*

**impedimenta**

(n.) im-ped-ih-MEN-tah—the equipment transported by
an army
*The troops gathered their impedimenta and began the
    day's march.*

**imperious**

(adj.) im-PEER-ee-uhs—domineering in a conceited manner;
overbearing
*Winifred dismissed the waiter with an imperious wave.*

**imperturbable**

(adj.) im-per-TUR-bah-bul—incapable of being upset
*All the best billiards players are imperturbable.*

**impetrate**

(v.) IM-pi-treyt—to attain by request
*The child impetrated another candy from his mother.*

**implacable**

(adj.) im-PLAK-a-bul—incapable of pacification, relentless

*The implacable boxer would not let his opponent rest.*

**imponderable**

(adj.) im-PON-der-a-bul—that cannot be evaluated or measured

*The poet says true love is imponderable.*

> Love is the only force capable of transforming
> an enemy into a friend.
>
> **—Martin Luther King Jr.**

**imprecate**

(v.) IM-prih-keyt—to curse or wish evil on

*Ian imprecated his boss, who made him work late on
Christmas Eve.*

**impuissant**

(n.) im-PWEE-suhnt—lacking strength; weak

*The school bully only picked on impuissant students in the
schoolyard.*

**in situ**

(adv. & adj.) in-SIH-too—in the original location or
placement

*Seeing artifacts in situ helps to learn about a new place.*

**inanition**

(n.) in-uh-NISH-uhn—the condition of emptiness

*After skipping breakfast, Darlene's inanition led to a decrease in
work performance.*

**incarnadine**

(adj.) in-KAHR-nah-dyn—dark red; crimson
*The bandage will be incarnadine after it encases the severe wound.*

**inchoate**

(adj.) in-KOH-it—incomplete or lacking full development
*The writer turned an inchoate idea into a four-hundred-page novel.*

**inchoative**

(adj.) in-KOH-uh-tiv—at the onset of, incipient
*The plan was still in its inchoative stages.*

**incongruous**

(adj.) in-KONG-groo-us—not harmonious; inconsonant
*The incongruous couple somehow stayed together for years.*

**incubus**

(n.) IN-kyoo-bus—a demon that haunts people in nightmares
*Donovan was not getting enough sleep because a recurring incubus was haunting his dreams.*

**inculpate**

(v.) in-KUHL-peyt—to accuse of a crime; incriminate
*Joe said if they reported him, he would inculpate them, too.*

**incunabulum**

(n.) in-kyoo-NAB-ya-lum—the early stages
*The IT expert worked in the computer industry since its incunabulum.*

**indefatigable**

(adj.) in-deh-FAT-i-guh-buhl—not giving in to fatigue; tireless
*The coach thanked the players for their indefatigable work in the playoffs.*

**indehiscent**

(adj.) in-dih-HIS-uhnt—not breaking open at maturity
*I attacked the walnut's indehiscent shell with a nutcracker.*

**indite**

(v.) in-DAYT—to compose
*Jack Kerouac indited* On the Road *on one continuous scroll of paper.*

**indolent**

(adj.) IN-doh-lint—persistently lethargic
*He was called an indolent boy because he never cleaned his room.*

**ineffable**

(adj.) in-EF-uh-bul—incapable of description
*The chef adored the ineffable aroma of the Italian white truffle.*

**ineluctable**

(adj.) in-i-LUHK-tuh-buhl—unavoidable
*Jason feared that more layoffs were ineluctable, despite his best efforts to prevent them.*

**inexpugnable**

(adj.) in-ex-SPUHG-nuh-bul—capable of withstanding any attack
*The fortress was deemed inexpugnable.*

**infra dig**

(adj.) IN-fruh-DIG—going against one's dignity
*Will considered washing the floor on his knees to be infra dig.*

**inglenook**

(n.) ING-guhl-nook—a secluded corner or spot near a fireplace
*During the winter, Victor enjoyed curling up with a good book in his inglenook.*

**ingravescent**

(adj.) in-gra-VES-ent—becoming increasingly harsh or serious
*The older woman had ingravescent lower back pain that made it difficult to walk.*

**ingurgitate**

(v.) in-GUR-jit-eyt—to devour greedily; acting as a glutton
*She scorned her husband for ingurgitating his dinner.*

**inimical**

(adj.) ih-NIM-ih-kul—unfriendly; hostile
*The inimical old man next door glared at neighbors who waved at him.*

**innervate**

(v.) in-NUR-vayt—to supply with nervous energy; rouse
*He innervated the crowd with a rousing speech.*

**innominate**

(adj.) in-NOM-in-ut—nameless
*The newborn remained innominate for a week as the parents argued over a name.*

**inquietude**

(n.) in-KWAY-i-tood—a feeling of restlessness
*He felt an inquietude until the job was done.*

**insalubrious**

(adj.) in-sah-LOO-bree-uss—unfavorable to health
*Without efforts to reverse damage done, air quality will continue to become increasingly insalubrious.*

**insouciant**

(adj.) in-SOO-see-ahnt—free from worry; carefree
*Overwhelmed by bills, work and everyday life, Olive yearned for the days of her insouciant youth.*

**inspissate**

(v.) in-SPIS-eyt—to produce density
*Emeril Lagasse inspissated the Cajun sauce to perfection.*

**instauration**

(n.) in-staw-REY-shuhn—renovation or revitalization
*They collected donations for the instauration of the Baghdad museum.*

**insuperable**

(adj.) in-SOOP-er-ah-bul—impossible to exceed or outdo
*Insuperable obstacles forced her to give up the chase.*

**intercalate**

(v.) in-TUR-kah-leyt—to interject between current layers
*The chef intercalated an extra layer of chocolate into the cake.*

**interdict**

(v.) IN-ter-dikt—to forbid or ban
*Joe's diet interdicted him from eating carbs.*

**interdigitate**

(v.) in-ter-DIJ-i-teyt—to interlock the fingers of each hand
*The old country road interdigitates with the woodland, winding around trees and streams.*

**internecine**

(adj.) in-tuhr-NES-een—pertaining to discord among a group
*Rock bands often split up over internecine.*

**interregnum**

(n.) in-tur-REG-num—a period of time between rulers
*The interregnum between Pope John Paul II and Pope Benedict XVI lasted about two weeks.*

**interstice**

(adj.) in-tur-STIS—an intervening space forming separation
*There was a narrow interstice between the two buildings.*

**intestate**

(adj.) in-TES-teyt—having made no will

*The intestate mother was constantly pressured by her children to make a will.*

> Parents who expect change in themselves as well as in their children, who accept it and find in it the joy as well as the pains of growth, are likely to be the happiest and most confident parents.
>
> —**Fred Rogers**

**intractable**

(adj.) in-TRAK-tah-bul—difficult to manage; stubborn

*The intractable child caused her mother grief.*

**introit**

(n.) IN-troh-it—the opening hymn of a religious service

*Andrew arrived at church just in time to hear the introit.*

**inure**

(v.) in-YOOR—to acclimate to hardship

*The sewer workers were inured to the foul stench.*

**invective**

(n.) in-VEK-tiv—an insulting expression

*Barry's invective consisted of many four-letter expletives.*

**inveigle**

(v.) in-VEY-guhl—to entice by flattery

*The gossip columnist inveigled the actress into granting him an interview.*

**inveterate**

(adj.) in-VET-er-it—strongly established in a habit

*The inveterate bus driver could practically drive the route with his eyes closed.*

**invidious**

(adj.) in-VID-ee-uhs—intended to cause animosity

*The celebrity's invidious comments were splashed across the tabloids the next day.*

**irenic**

(adj.) ay-REN-ik—usually promoting reconciliation or peace

*The teacher's irenic nature helped her quickly sort out schoolyard brawls.*

**irreproachable**

(adj.) eer-ee-PROH-chuh-bul—impossible to find fault with

*Her irreproachable conduct led to a promotion.*

# J

**jackanapes**

(n.) JAK-uh-neyps—a mischievous, impudent person
*Vivian ditched her blind date, who turned out to be a
jackanapes, before dessert.*

**jack-tar**

(n.) JAK-tahr—a mariner
*Jerry's dream of becoming a jack-tar vanished after seeing* The
Perfect Storm.

**jalopy**

(n.) juh-LOP-ee—a decrepit vehicle
*Jay finally took his jalopy to the junkyard.*

**jejune**

(adj.) jih-JOON—lacking significance; uninteresting
*After talking about office supplies for hours, Marge tried to
escape from her jejune co-worker June at the holiday party.*

**jeremiad**

(n.) jair-ah-MY-ahd—a disappointing lamentation
*Kelly felt exceedingly pessimistic after reading the jeremiad
regarding the state of society.*

**jerry-built**

(v.) JER-ee-bilt—to build in a cheap fashion
*The contractors jerry-built houses for years before they
were caught.*

**jetsam**

(n.) JET-suhm—goods cast overboard to lighten a vessel in distress

*The struggling company got rid of employees like jetsam.*

**jingoism**

(n.) JING-goh-iz-uhm—excessive nationalism or patriotism marked by a aggressive foreign policy

*The country's jingoism could easily spur an unnecessary war.*

**jocund**

(adj.) JOK-uhnd—joyous, cheery

*The man was always jocund, even in tough situations.*

**juju**

(n.) JOO-joo—an object revered for spiritual purposes

*Gerald brought a juju with him when he went to the casino.*

**junoesque**

(adj.) joo-noh-ESK—regal; relating to female beauty in honor of the goddess Juno

*Katrina possessed a junoesque presence that drew the attention of many.*

**juvenescent**

(adj.) joo-vuh-NES-uhnt—relating to youthful beauty

*She hoped the new skin cream would make her juvenescent.*

# K

**kakistocracy**

(n.) kak-ah-STOK-rah-see—leadership by the least qualified
*The kakistocracy crumbled not long after the leader was elected.*

> Ninety percent of the politicians give the
> other ten percent a bad reputation.
>
> **—Henry Kissinger**

**kapellmeister**

(n.) kah-pell-MY-ster—director of a musical group, especially
a choir
*The kapellmeister and his group were in high demand for
holiday festivities.*

**ken**

(n.) KEHN—range of understanding of a subject
*Bill has no ken of the female mind and is doomed to
remain single.*

**kerf**

(n.) KERF—the space made in wood by a cutting tool
*The logger made a kerf in the tree with his chainsaw.*

**kerfuffle**

(n.) kur-FUH-ful—a disorderly disturbance

*Mike caused a kerfuffle at the office when he unexpectedly quit.*

**kismet**

(n.) KIZ-met—destiny

*It was kismet that they met at the New Year's party and married a year later.*

**klatch**

(n.) KLATSH—a gathering for discussion, often over coffee

*Madison met her friends for a klatch at the coffeehouse.*

**knave**

(n.) NEYV—an untrustworthy person

*Dave, the office knave, was caught more than once stealing supplies.*

**kvetch**

(v.) KVECH—to chronically moan about life

*Nancy was tired of listening to her co-worker kvetch every morning about her commute.*

# L

**labile**

(adj.) LEY-bihl—open to change

*Kelly's labile personality made her prone to outside influence.*

**lachrymose**

(adj.) LAK-rih-mohs—given to crying

*Bob has been unusually lachrymose ever since his dog died.*

**laconic**

(adj.) lah-KON-ik—tersely expressive

*Frank's laconic replies usually coincided with Monday mornings.*

**lacuna**

(n.) lah-KYOO-nuh—a gap or discontinuity

*His good personality made up for the lacuna in his education.*

**lacustrine**

(adj.) lah-KUS-trin—having to do with a lake

*The researchers discovered many lacustrine organisms.*

**lagniappe**

(n.) LAN-yap—a bonus

*The TV infomercial offered a free set of steak knives as
a lagniappe.*

**lambent**

(adj.) LAM-behnt—touching lightly; flickering

*The lambent flames from the fireplace gave the room a
relaxing feel.*

**lancinate**

(v.) LAN-suh-neyt—to cut

*The sharp wind in the alleyway lancinated Hugo's skin.*

**languid**

(adj.) LANG-gwid—lacking spirit or energy

*The coach urged the languid players to pick up the pace.*

**lanuginous**

(adj.) luh-NOO-juh-nohs—covered with fluffy down or underhair

*The lanuginous newborn puppies were a big hit with the kids.*

**lapidary**

(n.) LAP-uh-dair-ee—one who cuts gems

*The lapidary leads several rockhounding field trips a year.*

**lassitude**

(n.) LAS-ihtood—extreme weariness

*Trisha, engulfed by a feeling of lassitude after her workout, decided that she deserved some Ben & Jerry's.*

**latitudinarian**

(adj.) lat-i-tood-n-AIR-ee-uhn—tolerant of many views

*My latitudinarian mother let me choose my own religion.*

> Without tolerance, our world turns into hell.
> —**Friedrich Durrenmatt**

**laudatory**

(adj.) LAW-duh-tawr-ee—praising, complimentary

*The company president gave a laudatory speech about the employees.*

**lea**

(n.) LEE—a plain of grass
*The cattle grazed in the lea on a still spring morning.*

**legerdemain**

(n.) lej-er-duh-MEYN—artful trickery
*The smooth-talking politician was elected through legerdemain, saying what people wanted to hear.*

**leiodermia**

(n.) lyo-DUR-mee-ah—skin with a lustrous quality
*Lawrence never used moisturizer because he had leiodermia.*

**lenitive**

(adj.) LEN-ih-tiv—softening, relieving pain
*The doctor prescribed a lenitive drug for the patient.*

**lenity**

(n.) LEN-ih-tee—a merciful or lenient act
*The judge was known for her lenity toward criminals.*

**lethologica**

(n.) leth-uh-LAW-jik-ah—lacking the ability to remember a word
*The office worker was struck by lethologica while trying to submit a word of the day.*

**lilliputian**

(adj.) lil-ih-PYOO-shuhn—insignificant, or petty
*My everyday burdens seem lilliputian when compared with the problems that people have in third-world countries.*

**liminal**

(adj.) LIM-uh-nl—bordering on the threshold of sensory perception
*The audience struggled to hear the shy karaoke singer's liminal voice.*

**limpid**

(adj.) LIM-pid—clear

*They could see fish clearly through the limpid water of the stream.*

**linguaphile**

(n.) LING-gwuh-fayl—a lover of words and linguistic knowledge

*Larry the linguaphile loves to play Scrabble.*

**lippitude**

(n.) LIP-ih-tood—discomfort or bleariness of the eyes

*Leah suffered from lippitude the morning after her bachelorette party.*

**liripipe**

(n.) LIR-ee-pyp—a cord or strip attached to a hood or headdress

*The medieval academic enjoyed playing practical jokes on his partner, often hiding his liripipe around the castle.*

**lissome**

(adj.) LIS-um—nimble, flexible or agile

*The gymnast has a lissome, slender form.*

**literatim**

(adv.) lit-uh-REY-tim—literally, letter for letter

*She transcribed the ancient text literatim into her journal for future translation.*

**lithic**

(adj.) LITH'-ik—relating to, or consisting of stone

*Michelangelo's David is one of the most celebrated pieces of lithic art.*

**littoral**

(adj.) LIH-tuh-rul—relating to the shores of a body of water
*When Peter turned sixty-five, he bought a littoral home and spent his retired years sailing and fishing.*

**logorrhea**

(n.) law-guh-REE-uh—excessive, or compulsive talkativeness
*Tom's beautifully prepared speech turned into logorrhea when he proposed to Tammy.*

> Wise men talk because they have something to say. Fools talk because they have to say something.
>
> **—Plato**

**logy**

(n.) LOH-gee—lacking mental or physical vigor; lethargic
*The logy professor shuffled around the room, mumbling incoherently.*

**loutish**

(adj.) LOU-tish—awkward or clumsy; oafish
*The grimy bar was full of loutish brutes.*

**lucre**

(n.) LOO-ker—financial achievement or gain
*She turned down the contract and said it did not offer enough lucre.*

**lucubrate**

(v.) LOO-koo-breyt—to cram or work at night
*James knew that he must lucubrate for many hours before he could sleep.*

**luculent**

(adj.) LOO-kyuh-luhnt—easily comprehended
*Allen's writing is so luculent that anyone can comprehend his books.*

**Lucullan**

(adj.) loo-KULL-un—extravagant, opulent
*Lucy planned a Lucullan feast for Mardi Gras, featuring Cajun foods, king cakes, and cocktails.*

**lugubrious**

(adj.) loo-GOO-bree-uhs—gloomy, mournful, depressing
*The basset hound's lugubrious expression belies its affectionate temperament.*

**lummox**

(n.) LUHM-uhks—an inept, inelegant person
*His boss called him a lummox after he stumbled into a wall and dropped his files.*

**lumpen**

(adj.) LUHM-puhn—disenfranchised or dispossessed, low
*Kara's office indiscretions dragged her down to lumpen status.*

**lunker**

(n.) LUHNG-ker—anything considered unusually large in size
*The trout he caught on the fishing trip was a real lunker.*

**lycanthropy**

(n.) lay-KAN-thruh-pee—the delusional state of mind in which someone imagines himself to be a wolf or other animal *Michael J. Fox's character in* Teen Wolf *discovers that lycanthropy runs in his family.*

> Lawrence Talbot (Lon Chaney Jr): "Soon the moon will rise and I'll turn into a wolf."
>
> Wilbur (Lou Costello): "You and twenty million other guys."
>
> —*Abbott & Costello Meet Frankenstein* (1948)

## macabre

(adj.) mah-KAH-bruh—gruesome and horrifying; ghastly
*Mitch made the mistake of taking his blind date to a*
  *macabre movie.*

## machinate

(v.) MAK-uh-neyt—to plan with evil intent
*The conspirators machinated in the dark alley.*

## maculate

(adj.) MAK-yoo-lut—stained, tarnished, or impure
*The rugby player's shirt was maculate with mud splatters.*

## madding

(adj.) MAD-ing—acting insane or frenzied
*They found a place on the beach far from the madding crowd.*

## maelstrom

(n.) MEYL-strum—a tumultuous or disorderly situation
*The residents evacuated the city to avoid being caught in the*
  *maelstrom of war.*

## maffick

(v.) MAF-ik—to celebrate loudly in public
*The graduating class planned to maffick after the final exam.*

## magniloquent

(adj.) mag-NIL-oh-kwent—speaking pompously
*He was magniloquent, but he never followed up on his plan.*

**mahout**

(n.) muh-HOUT—elephant keeper

*Our sightseeing safari was led by a mahout who taught us all about his pet elephant.*

**majuscule**

(adj.) mah-JUHS-kyool—large or capital letters

*Mary's e-mail, written in majuscule letters, was not a happy one.*

**malady**

(n.) MAL-uh-dee—an undesirable illness

*Some people would say that an obsession with perfection is a modern malady.*

**malarkey**

(n.) muh-LAHR-kee—silly talk

*The employees thought Nick's presentation was a bunch of malarkey.*

**malingerer**

(n.) muh-LING-ger-er—one that fakes sicknesses to avoid work

*Fridays are tempting days to be a malingerer and call in sick.*

**malodorous**

(adj.) mal-OH-duhr-uhs—having a putrid scent

*Mark took one whiff of his malodorous meal and decided to order takeout.*

**manacle**

(n.) MAN-uh-kull—handcuffs

*Susan was placed in manacles after police found drugs in her pocket.*

**manse**

(n.) MANS—a large residence of a parson

*The two-story manse featured a library and a banquet-size dining room.*

**mansuetude**

(n.) MAN-swi-tood—the state of being gentle
*Amy's mansuetude made her pleasant to be around.*

**manumit**

(v.) man-yuh-MIT—to release from servitude
*The newly passed law led the government to manumit scores
of slaves.*

**marplot**

(n.) MAR-plot—one who interferes
*No one wanted to make any deals with Jim, who has the
reputation of being a marplot.*

**martinet**

(n.) mar-tin-ET—a stern authoritarian
*The basketball coach was such a martinet that his players grew
to hate him.*

> No one is born hating another person
> because of the color of his skin, or his back-
> ground, or his religion. People must learn
> to hate, and if they can learn to hate, they can
> be taught to love, for love comes more
> naturally to the human heart than its opposite.
>
> **—Nelson Mandela**

**masticate**

(v.) MAS-tih-keyt—to chew
*Rudy's mother taught him that he should masticate his food
exactly twenty-four times before swallowing.*

**matriculate**

(v.) mah-TRIK-yuh-leyt—to enroll in college

*My son plans to matriculate at Harvard following graduation from high school.*

**matutinal**

(adj.) mah-TOOT-n-ul—occurring in the morning

*Eating oatmeal and drinking coffee was part of Jacqui's matutinal process at work.*

**maunder**

(v.) MON-duhr—to ramble foolishly

*The newly married couple would maunder for hours about love.*

**mawkish**

(adj.) MAW-kish—overly sentimental

*My mawkish grandmother's house is overflowing with knickknacks that she cannot bear to throw away.*

**mealy-mouthed**

(adj.) MEE-lee-mowthd—devious, avoiding the use of simple, direct language

*The mealy-mouthed TV reporter presented viewers with a jumble of biased jargon.*

**melanophobia**

(n.) me-la-noh-FOH-bee-uh—trepidation of the color black

*Mark, who has melanophobia, shuddered at the sight of the black sweater he received as a gift.*

**melioration**

(n.) meel-yuh-REY-shun—the state of improvement

*The increased funds represent a great melioration for the research project.*

**mellifluous**

(adj.) MEH-lif-loo-uhs—characterized by sweet flow

*The massage therapist turned on some mellifluous music to help her client relax.*

**mendacious**

(adj.) men-DEY-shuhs—characterized by habitual lying

*Mandy was sick of hearing her cheating husband's mendacious drivel.*

**mendicant**

(n.) MEN-di-kuhnt—a panhandler

*Many big cities have mendicants who accost people for change.*

**mentation**

(n.) men-TEY-shun—mental activity

*Studies show high levels of mentation during the deepest phase of sleep.*

**mephitic**

(adj.) meh-FIT-ik—unbearable aromatically

*The mephitic odors of the city streets were unbearable.*

**mephitis**

(n.) meh-FY-tiss—a disgusting scent

*A mephitis pervaded the seedy motel room.*

**meretricious**

(adj.) mer-ih-TRISH-uhs—tacky; flashy

*The meretricious decorations on the neighbor's house were an eyesore.*

**metier**

(n.) met-YAY—an area of excellence; forte

*Bill, who studied chemistry in college, found his metier in the laboratory.*

**miasma**

(n.) may-AZ-muh—toxic or perilous atmosphere
*The drug user fell into a miasma of paranoia.*

**milksop**

(n.) MILK-sop—a weak person
*Jose considered himself a milksop because he was too timid to stand up to his boss.*

**milliner**

(n.) MIL-uh-ner—one who fabricates hats for sale
*Coco Chanel began her fashion career as a milliner, opening up a hat shop in the early 1900s.*

**milquetoast**

(n.) MILK-tohst—an overly unassertive person, a milksop
*The milquetoast did not have an answer to his overbearing wife.*

**minacious**

(adj.) mih-NAY-shuss—causing alarm; ominous
*The minacious clouds did little to spoil the family reunion at the park.*

**minatory**

(adj.) MIN-uh-tor-ee—intended to menace
*The man on trial gave minatory looks to the prosecutor.*

**minify**

(v.) MIN-uh-fy—to minimize or lessen
*He tried to minify his competitor's achievements.*

**misanthropic**

(adj.) mis-uhn-THROP-ik—having a general hatred for mankind
*Because of the sneer on his face, everybody thought he was misanthropic.*

**misfeasance**

(n.) mis-FEE-zahnts—wrongful execution of legal authority

*The public official was found guilty of misfeasance after voting for the unconstitutional bill.*

**misoneism**

(n.) mis-oh-NEE-ism—hatred of change

*The company's bankruptcy was a direct result of the president's misoneism.*

**mnemonics**

(n.) nih-MON-iks—a device aimed at improving memory

*The students used mnemonics to study for the exam.*

**modicum**

(n.) MOD-ih-kuhm—a little bit

*A modicum of good sense goes a long way.*

**moiety**

(n.) MOY-uh-tee—one of two equivalent portions, a half

*After splitting the cupcake with her friend, Nina quickly ate her moiety.*

**mollify**

(v.) MOL-uh-fay—to soften or pacify in temperament

*She sang a lullaby to mollify the wailing baby.*

**monition**

(n.) muh-NISH-un—an official warning; usually legal

*The court's monition of the trial caused anxiety in the recipient.*

**monoglot**

(adj.) MON-oh-glaht—fluent in just one language

*The monoglot travelers had trouble asking for directions during their world tour.*

**monomania**

(n.) mohn-oh-MEY-nee-ah—obsessive interest in something
*His wife said his monomania with football had to end.*

**monopsony**

(n.) moh-NOP-soh-nee—a market condition in which there is only one buyer
*The state's farm monopsony gouged the struggling producers.*

**moppet**

(n.) MOP-it—a little boy or girl
*The moppet displayed such innocence when he played outside with his friends.*

**mordacious**

(adj.) mor-DEY-shus—sarcastically critical or scathing
*Tony was difficult to talk to because of his mordacious tendencies.*

**mordant**

(adj.) MAWR-dant—caustic, biting
*Penelope's mordant humor is often hurtful.*

**mores**

(n.) MAWR-eyz—customs of a group
*"Casual Fridays" were looked down upon as a relaxation of traditional office mores.*

**morganatic**

(adj.) mawr-gah-NAT-ik—of a marriage involving a noble and a commoner
*The son of a morganatic marriage can never be king.*

**moribund**

(adj.) MAWR-uh-bund—on the verge of death
*The moribund man rewrote his will.*

> Death is a very dull, dreary affair, and
> my advice to you is to have nothing
> whatsoever to do with it.
>
> —Somerset Maugham

**mot juste**

(n.) moh JOOST—the most suitable word or term
*The comedian found the mot juste to describe the target of his joke.*

**mucky-muck**

(n.) MUHK-ee-MUHK—an arrogant person
*"You're such a mucky-muck," the caller said to the pompous radio talk show therapist.*

**mucronate**

(adj.) MYOO-kroh-nit—bearing an abrupt point
*The bird used its mucronate beak to peck for worms.*

**mufti**

(n.) MUHF-tee—civilian clothing worn by someone who is usually in uniform
*No one had ever seen the commander in mufti.*

**mulct**

(v.) MUHLKT—to gain money by extortion or other illegal practices
*The e-mail scammers mulcted millions of dollars from gullible people.*

**multifarious**

(adj.) muhl-tih-FEHR-ee-uhs—varying in parts or forms
*The company had a multifarious group of employees.*

**multitudinous**

(adj.) mul-tih-TOOD-n-uhs—happening or existing in great number

*Parents face multitudinous challenges when raising children.*

**munificent**

(adj.) myoo-NIF'-ih-sint—known for great generosity

*Shelly's munificent grandmother always gave her big gifts.*

**muzzy**

(adj.) MUHZ-ee—distracted, perplexed

*Marge dragged her muzzy eyes away from her wineglass and tried to focus on what her boss was saying.*

**myopia**

(n.) may-OH'-pee-uh—shortsightedness

*Mental myopia kept Karen from saving for her future.*

**myrmecology**

(n.) mur-mih-KOL-uh-jee—type of entomology concentrated on ants

*Tory's interest in myrmecology vanished as soon as her ant farm cracked open and the creatures infested her bedroom.*

**myrmidon**

(n.) mur-mih-don—a devoted follower

*He sent his myrmidons to do his dirty work.*

**mythomania**

(n.) mith-uh-MEY-nee-uh—excessive lying

*Megan's mythomania always got her in trouble.*

# N

**nabob**

(n.) NEY-bob—a person of great wealth and influence
*The exclusive community was home to many local nabobs.*

**nadir**

(n.) NEY-deer—the lowest point
*The team reached its nadir after losing twelve games in a row.*

**nascent**

(adj.) NEY-suhnt—beginning to exist; emerging
*We had difficulty getting reservations at the nascent restaurant.*

**natal**

(adj.) NEYT-l—relating to a human birth
*Wendy celebrated her natal day by eating ice cream for breakfast.*

> A diplomat is a man who always remembers a woman's birthday but never remembers her age.
>
> **—Robert Frost**

**natty**

(adj.) NAT-ee—clean-cut attire
*The natty salesman impressed the client with his professional appearance.*

**nebbishy**

(adj.) NEB-ish-ee—timid, ineffectual

*That nebbishy guy will never get a promotion.*

**nemorous**

(adj.) NEM-oh-rous—arboreal

*The cozy cottage was tucked away in a nemorous setting.*

**nescience**

(n.) NESH-uhns—deficiency of knowledge

*He had to confess nescience in local politics.*

**nescient**

(adj.) NESH-uhnt—ignorant, uneducated

*The arts student was nescient of science.*

**netiquette**

(n.) NET-h-keht—the rules of protocol applying to the Internet.

*E-mails written in all caps are a breach of netiquette.*

**nettle**

(v.) NET-l—to annoy

*The child nettled the babysitter with his constant complaining.*

**nictitate**

(v.) NIK-tih-teyt—to blink

*Carol nictitated at the attractive man sitting next to her on the bus.*

**nidification**

(n.) NID-uh-fi-KAY-shun—the act of constructing a nest

*The bird-watchers admired the sparrow's nidification technique.*

**niff**

(n.) NIF—a repulsive smell

*The spilled gas caused such a niff that Hilary showered as soon as she arrived home from work.*

**nimiety**

(n.) nih-MAY-ih-tee—surplus or overabundance

*The concept of having a nimiety of money did not exist to the poor college student.*

**nobble**

(v.) NAHB-uhl—to swindle or cheat

*Security caught the poker player trying to nobble.*

**nodus**

(n.) NOH-dus—a strenuous predicament

*Tom faced a nodus when his car broke down on the highway.*

**noetic**

(adj.) noh-ET-ik—pertaining to reason

*He went to the library to develop his noetic ability.*

**nolens volens**

(adv.) NOH-lenz VOH-lenz—whether eager or reluctant

*Growing up in the city forced Greg to become the social director for his friends, nolens volens.*

**nonage**

(n.) NON-ij—a period of being immature

*The awkward mistakes of my youth only enriched my nonage.*

**nonagenarian**

(n.) non-uh-juh-NAIR-ee-uhn—a person between the ages of ninety and one hundred

*The nursing home was full of nonagenarians.*

> Old age isn't so bad when you consider the alternative.
>
> **—Maurice Chevalier**

**nonesuch**

(n.) NUHN-suhch—a person or thing that is so superior it has no rivals

*Paco de Lucia is a nonesuch in the world of flamenco music.*

**nonet**

(n.) NOH-net—a musical ensemble comprised of nine people

*The nonet's rich and colorful combinations resembled the sound of a chamber orchestra.*

**nosegay**

(n.) NOHZ-gey—a little cluster of flowers

*The old man surprised his wife with a nosegay on their fiftieth anniversary.*

**nosologist**

(n.) no-SOL-uh-jist—one who classifies diseases

*The nosologist rarely deals with noses, as most deaths are not nasal related.*

**nostrum**

(n.) NOS-truhm—a fake medicine with questionable efficacy

*John was duped into buying a nostrum he thought would cure his illness.*

**nudnik**

(n.) NOOD-nik—a bothersome pest or bore

*His younger brother was a real nudnik.*

**numen**

(n.) NOO-mun—a locally presiding spirit

*They believed that the numen of the house would keep it safe.*

**numinous**

(adj.) NOO-mah-nuhs—spiritual

*Looking out over the mountains was a numinous experience.*

**numismatist**

(n.) noo-MIZ-mah-tist—someone who researches coins

*The numismatist was hired by the Independent Coin Grading Co. as a coin grader.*

**nutation**

(n.) noo-TEY-shuhn—the act of spastic head nodding

*There was much nutation during the president's speech.*

**nyctophobia**

(n.) nik-tuh-FOH-bee-uh—an irregular fear of night or darkness

*Nick dealt with his nyctophobia by putting a night-light in every room of his house.*

# O

**obdurate**

(adj.) OB-doo-rit—unfeeling, hardened
*Greg's obdurate demeanor around the office made him unapproachable.*

**obfuscate**

(v.) OB-fuh-skeyt—to muddle
*Ken's excessive verbiage in the work papers obfuscated the overall point.*

**objurgate**

(v.) OB-jer-geyt—to harshly reprimand
*Tired of her boss's objurgating her work, Shelby packed up her desk and left.*

**oblation**

(n.) ob-BLAY-shuhn—an offering for a church
*When Oliver won the lottery he offered oblations to the local food bank.*

**obloquy**

(n.) OB-luh-kwee—abusive language
*The visiting team had to deal with obloquies from the hometown crowd.*

**obnubilate**

(v.) ob-NOO-buh-leyt—to blur the meaning of; confuse
*Money obnubilated the businessman's morals.*

**obsequies**

(n.) OB-sih-kwees—rites of the deceased at funerals

*The bishop's obsequies were held in the cathedral.*

**obsequious**

(adj.) uhb-SEE-kwee-uhs—showing complacence in servitude

*The obsequious servants scurried to fulfill their king's command.*

**obtund**

(v.) ub-TUHND—to dull down

*They obtunded the gory storylines from the original fairy tales.*

**occlude**

(v.) uh-KLOOD—to obstruct

*The heavy blinds occluded all sunlight from the room.*

**ochlocracy**

(n.) ok-LOK-rah-see—authority or rule by the mob

*The Jacobin rule of France degenerated into an ochlocracy.*

**ochlophobia**

(n.) ok-luh-FOH-bee-uh—an irregular fear of crowds

*Since Shelby has ocholophobia, she likes to start her holiday
shopping in September to avoid the crowds.*

**octothorpe**

(n.) OK-to-thorp—the character #

*In the 1960s, Bell Labs introduced two new keys on its
touch-tone telephone—the octothorpe and the asterisk.*

**odious**

(adj.) OH-dee-uhs—worthy of hatred

*Jane gave her notice after her odious boss berated her in front of
her co-workers.*

**odontalgia**

(n.) oh-don-TAL-juh—a pain or ache in a tooth

*Due to his odontalgia, Trent was unable to drink any cold liquids.*

**oikology**

(n.) oy-KOLL-uh-jee—the science or analysis of housekeeping

*Martha Stewart has raised oikology to an art form.*

**oleaginous**

(adj.) oh-lee-AJ-uh-nuhs—oily, insincere in flattery

*He received an oleaginous letter of apology from the company.*

**olio**

(n.) OH-lee-o—a miscellaneous mixture

*George gave his wife an olio of chocolates for Valentine's Day.*

**omnifarious**

(adj.) awm-nih-FEHYR-ee-uss—of all varying forms

*She had an omnifarious knowledge of poetry.*

**omphaloskepsis**

(n.) om-fuh-loh-SKEP-sis—Focus on one's navel

*Whenever you finish your omphaloskepsis, let's talk about our actual strategy.*

**oniomania**

(n.) oh-nee-oh-MEY-nee-uh—irrepressible urge to purchase things

*Some say society encourages oniomania.*

**onychophagy**

(n.) on-ih-KOF-uh-jee—habitual biting of the fingernails

*George's onychophagy emerged whenever he watched stressful baseball games.*

**opalesce**

(v.) oh-pah-LESS—to reflect or exhibit iridescence

*The tips of the waves opalesced under the shining sun.*

**operose**

(adj.) OP-uh-roes—involving much labor

*Tim was told to take a break from any operose work after he passed out on the job.*

**opine**

(v.) oh-PAYN—to state an opinion, to suppose

*She opined that the stock market would finish higher today.*

**opprobrium**

(n.) uh-PROH-bree-uhm—disgrace caused by shameful conduct

*An opprobrium can become a catalyst for a celebrity's career.*

**oppugnant**

(adj.) uh-PUHG-nuhnt—hostile or antagonistic

*The oppugnant activists disrupted the economic summit.*

**oriflamme**

(n.) OR-uh-flam—an inspiring banner or symbol

*The soldier held the flag as an oriflamme as he led the troops into battle.*

**ornery**

(adj.) OR-ner-ee—having an irritable or unpleasant disposition

*She refused to work with such an ornery group of people.*

**ornithological**

(adj.) awr-nuh-thuh-LOJ-ih-kuhl—of or relating to the division of zoology that deals with birds

*Owen's ornithological interests are illustrated by his extensive library of bird books.*

**ornithopter**

(n.) awr-nuh-THOP-ter—an aircraft that uses flapping wings to fly

*Steve says he piloted an ornithopter when he was in the army.*

**ort**

(n.) ORT—a scrap or morsel

*Margie was punished by her mother for leaving an ort of food on her plate at dinner.*

**orthoepy**

(n.) awr-THOH-uhp-ee—the study of the correct pronunciation of words

*Orthoepy was irrelevant to the Scrabble champion.*

**oscitancy**

(n.) OS-ih-tuhn-see—lethargy or drowsiness

*Oscitancy was prevalent at the sales meeting.*

**otiose**

(adj.) OH-shee-ohss—lazy, idle or sluggish

*He was feeling otiose the day after the holiday party.*

**outré**

(adj.) oo-TRAY—outside the limits of what is proper; bizarre

*The fashion label was known for its outré designs.*

**owlish**

(adj.) OW-lish—appearing solemn and wise, characteristic of an owl

*The owlish fortune teller was cloaked in an air of mystery.*

# P

**pabulum**

(n.) PAB-yuh-lum—food providing nourishment
*On an empty stomach, even crackers can serve as pabulum.*

**pachydermatous**

(adj.) pak-i-DUR-muh-tuhs—thick-skinned; unfeeling
*The pachydermatous old man softened at the sight of his granddaughter.*

**paean**

(n.) PEE-ahn—a song or writing expressing great praise
*Beethoven's Fidelio is a paean to married love.*

**paladin**

(n.) PAL-uh-din—a champion of a noble cause
*Bobby was considered a paladin for his effort in securing office slippers for employees.*

**palaver**

(v.) pah-LAV-er—a lengthy discussion or conference
*There was always a palaver about where to go for the department lunch.*

**palliate**

(v.) PAL-ee-ayt—to make less severe or intense; alleviate
*The boss tried to palliate the situation by cracking jokes.*

**panacea**

(n.) pan-uh-SEE-uh—a universal cure
*The therapist believes that talking about one's problems is the panacea for a troubled mind.*

**pandiculation**

(n.) pan-dik-yoo-LEY-shuhn—the feat of stretching oneself
*Gwen could have watched TV all day in a state of unending pandiculation, but guilt dragged her weary body to the gym.*

**panegyric**

(n.) pan-ih-JIR-ik—a grand writing or speech in praise of someone
*The English major wrote an ornate panegyric to the poet.*

**pangram**

(n.) PAN-gruhm—a sentence using every letter of the alphabet
*"Quick wafting zephyrs vex bold Jim" is a pangram.*

**panoptic**

(adj.) pan-OP-tik—encompassing everything in one view
*The panoptic view from the top of the mountain is worth the hike.*

**pari passu**

(adv.) PAIR-ee PASS-oo—at an equal pace or progression
*The new shares will rank pari passu in all respects with the existing shares.*

**parlous**

(adj.) PAHR-luhs—dangerous
*The adventure racers faced a parlous journey through the mountains.*

> *The optimist sees opportunity in every danger; the pessimist sees danger in every opportunity.*
>
> —**Winston Churchill**

## parsimonious

(adj.) pahr-suh-MOH-nee-uhs—overly frugal with money
*The bank's board was parsimonious with its loan approvals.*

## parsimony

(n.) PAHR-suh-moh-nee—excessive frugality
*Buying a shirt for more than ten dollars was a difficult decision for Lynn, who is the epitome of parsimony.*

## partitive

(adj.) PAHR-tih-tiv—dividing into parts
*The furniture played a partitive role in the open-concept house.*

## parturient

(adj.) pahr-TOOR-ee-uhnt—on the verge of bearing young
*Maura didn't want to take any drugs during childbirth, but then the parturient pangs began.*

## parure

(n.) pah-ROOR—a set of jewelry that matches
*The princess wore a stunning parure to the banquet.*

## parvenu

(n.) PAHR-veh-noo—a person who has gained wealth or position but not the conventionally appropriate social standing to match.
*The parvenu used his lottery winnings to gain entry into New York society.*

**passel**

(n.) PASS-uhl—a group with an imprecise number

*A passel of fans followed the pop star wherever he went.*

**pastiche**

(n.) pah-STEESH—a jumbled medley

*The band played a pastiche of music to try to please everyone.*

**pate**

(n.) PEYT—top or crown of one's head

*The man bought a toupee for his pate.*

**paucity**

(n.) PAW-sih-tee—scarce in quantity

*Residents were not allowed to use their sprinklers because of water paucity.*

**pavid**

(adj.) PAV-id—exhibiting fear, frightened

*The pavid employee will never ask for a raise.*

**peccadillo**

(n.) pek-uh-DIL-oh—a minor sin or wrongdoing

*Mark was ashamed of the slightest peccadillo because he is a perfectionist.*

The only difference between the saint and the sinner is that every saint has a past, and every sinner has a future.

—Oscar Wilde

**peccant**

(adj.) PEK-unt—in violation of a rule, guilty of transgression
*The peccant man prayed for redemption.*

**peccavi**

(n.) pe-KAH-wee—a confession of guilt
*Betty's affair was the subject of her peccavi to her husband.*

**pecksniffian**

(adj.) pek-SNIF-ee-an—hypocritical under a veil of benevolence
*The pecksniffian organization pocketed cash it collected for
 charity.*

**peculate**

(v.) PEK-yoo-leyt—to embezzle or take dishonestly
*The accountant peculated thousands of dollars from her clients.*

**pecuniary**

(adj.) pek-KYOO-nee-ehr-ee—concerning money
*There were many pecuniary considerations involved in the
 transaction.*

**pedagogic**

(adj.) ped-uh-GOJ-ik—relating to teaching or education
*The teacher used the computer as a pedagogic tool.*

**pejorative**

(adj.) peh-JAWR-uh-tiv—Tending to belittle; effecting
derogatively
*Devi slapped Dennis across the face after he made a pejorative
 comment about her outfit.*

**pelf**

(n.) PELF—Money or riches, especially when regarded
negatively
*Donald's pursuit of pelf strained his marriage and his health.*

**pell-mell**

(adv.) PEL-MEL—in a recklessly hurried manner
*The troops charged pell-mell into battle.*

**pellucid**

(adj.) peh-LOO-sid—transparent, clear
*Frank watched the tropical fish swim by him in the pellucid ocean.*

**pensile**

(adj.) PEN-sayl—dangling loosely, suspended
*The bird's pensile nest was clearly seen from the window by the tree.*

**pepo**

(n.) PEE-poh—any fruit of the gourd family, having a hard skin and plentiful seeds
*The open-air market had a large variety of pepos.*

**perambulate**

(v.) per-AM-byuh-leyt—to walk about, traverse through
*Fanny perambulated around the lake every morning.*

**percipient**

(adj.) per-SIP-ee-ent—capable of keen perception
*The percipient filmmaker was hailed as a genius.*

**perdurable**

(adj.) per-DUR-uh-bul—characterized by extreme durability
*Both John and Joan made sacrifices for their perdurable marriage which lasted into their nineties.*

**peremptory**

(adj.) puh-REMP-toh-ree—not allowing for debate; final
*A nervous hush swept over the boardroom following the CEO's peremptory remarks.*

**perfervid**

(adj.) per-FER-vid—impassioned or fervent

*Perfervid patriotism and fireworks are a dangerous combination on the Fourth of July.*

**perfidious**

(adj.) per-FID-ee-uhs—deliberately deceitful

*The perfidious salesman sold the broken stereo to the unsuspecting woman.*

**perfidy**

(n.) PER-fih-dee—intentional violation of faith or trust

*The supporters awoke to the leader's perfidy and turned against him.*

**perforce**

(adv.) per-FAWRS—by necessity of circumstance

*We will perforce be ordering in tonight because there is no food in the house.*

**perfunctory**

(adj.) per-FUNK-tuh-ree—performed out of duty; lacking interest or enthusiasm

*Pam fell asleep while listening to the perfunctory report on the company's revenue.*

**pericope**

(n.) puh-RIK-uh-pee—selection from a literary work

*The church service included a sermon from the priest and a pericope from the Bible.*

**peripatetic**

(adj.) per-ih-pah-TET-ik—ambling or traveling about

*The salesman grew tired of his peripatetic career.*

**permafrost**

(n.) PUR-muh-frawst—enduringly frozen subsoil
*Permafrost is commonly found in Alaska and northern parts of Canada.*

**pernicious**

(adj.) per-NISH-uhs—causing harm
*They spread pernicious rumors around the office to get her fired.*

**perquisite**

(n.) PER-kwuh-zit—a benefit received on top of standard salary or wages
*The restaurant manager received free meals as a perquisite.*

**perseverate**

(v.) per-SEV-uh-reyt—to repeat an action redundantly
*The boy perseverated in his demand for ice cream.*

**persiflage**

(n.) PER-suh-flahzh—light banter
*She was bored to tears by her date's endless persiflage.*

**perspicacious**

(adj.) per-spi-KEY-shuhs—insightful, wise
*Richard said the readers were perspicacious and would notice an error.*

**pertinacious**

(adj.) pur-tn-EY-shuhs—stubborn in course of action
*The pertinacious dog wouldn't stop begging for food.*

**peruke**

(n.) peh-rook—a male wig common in the seventeenth and eighteenth centuries
*Larry, dressed as King Louis XIV for Halloween, pulled his powdered peruke into a ponytail.*

---

**pestiferous**

(adj.) pes-TIF-uh-ruhs—morally evil or troublesome
*The neighbors had trouble selling their home because of the
abundance of pestiferous gangs in the area.*

> When choosing between two evils, I always
> like to try the one I've never tried before.
>
> —Mae West

**petard**

(n.) peh-TAHRD—an explosive device used to blow open doors
or walls
*The lock was so thick that Vince had to use a petard on it so he
could get inside the gate.*

**petrous**

(adj.) PE-truhs—resembling the hardness of rock or stone
*The old man's petrous heart softened a bit when the neighbor
brought over holiday cookies.*

**pettifoggery**

(n.) PET-ee-FAWG-er-ee—arguments over petty matters
*The debate was dominated by annoying pettifoggery.*

**pettish**

(adj.) PET-ish—ill-tempered, showing irritation
*Monday mornings always made Dominic pettish.*

**phaeton**

(n.) FEY-ton—a vintage four-wheeled carriage from the
nineteenth century
*The tourists took a ride through town in a vintage phaeton.*

**phatic**

(adj.) FAH-tik—conveying sociability instead of informational speech

*The townsfolk greeted each other with such phatic phrases as, "Good day!"*

**philippic**

(n.) fuh-LIP-ik—a denunciating outburst

*The lawmaker's philippic was full of attacks on his rival.*

**philistine**

(n.) FIL-ih-steen—one that is generally disdainful of intellectual or artistic values

*Bob is a philistine, and therefore refuses to spend time at art galleries.*

**philomath**

(n.) FIL-oh-math—one that loves learning; a scholar

*While most children demand toys for Christmas, this little philomath only wanted books.*

**philter**

(n.) FIL-ter—a magic potion, usually used for purposes of love

*They named the song "Love Potion No. 9" because "Philter No. 9" didn't have the same ring to it.*

**phlegmatic**

(adj.) fleg-MAT-ik—apathetic; displaying lack of excitement

*No sign of emotion appeared on Greg's phlegmatic face.*

**physiognomy**

(n.) fiz-ee-OG-nah-mee—the process of judging a person's character from facial features

*The CEO interviewed each candidate face-to-face, using physiognomy as a criterion.*

**pica**

(n.) PAY-kuh—an irregular craving for inedible substances, such as dirt or chalk
*Paul, who suffers from pica, was ashamed of his urges to eat glue.*

> Leo Bloom (Gene Wilder): "Actors are not animals! They're human beings!"
>
> Max Bialystock (Zero Mostel): "They are? Have you ever eaten with one?"
>
> —*The Producers,* 1968

**picaresque**

(adj.) pik-uh-RESK—characteristic of rogue figures
*The storyteller regaled the crowd with his picaresque tales.*

**picaroon**

(n.) pik-uh-ROON—a criminal
*The politically unstable country was overrun by picaroons.*

**pinniped**

(n.) PIN-uh-ped—mammal with limbs adapted for aquatic life
*Some scientists put pinnipeds, such as the seal, in the same taxonomic group as dogs.*

**piquant**

(adj.) pee-KAHNT—pleasantly stimulating or sharp, often in taste
*Some cheese becomes sharper and more piquant with age.*

**piscivorous**

(adj.) pih-SIV-ahr-us—routinely eating fish

*Otters, strictly piscivorous animals, eat mainly cichlids because they're easy fish to catch.*

**plaguy**

(adj.) PLEY-gee—annoying, irritating

*Lynn was unable to do her work due to a plaguy sound coming from the vents above her desk.*

**plangent**

(adj.) PLAN-juhnt—reverberating loudly

*She detested her roommate's plangent piano-playing.*

**platitude**

(n.) PLAT-ih-tood—banal or trite ideas

*Joey's new book began with such originality but quickly dissolved into platitude.*

**platitudinarian**

(n.) plat-ih-tood-n-AIR-ee-uhn—one who constantly speaks in dull truisms

*Beth was so bored by the platitudinarian sitting next to her that she began to play with her food.*

**plaudits**

(n.) PLAW-dits—demonstrations of approval

*The new CEO earned the plaudits of the shareholders.*

**plausive**

(adj.) PLAW-ziv—showing support

*The mayor received many plausive responses to his proposal.*

**pleach**

(v.) PLEETCH—to interweave or entangle (especially branches)

*The gardener pleached the vines along the fence.*

**pleonasm**

(n.) PLEE-oh-na-zem—a redundancy in speech or writing
*Ralph Wiggum is well known for his hilarious pleonasms.*

**plication**

(n.) play-KEY-shun—the act of folding materials
*She developed great plication skills while working at the clothing store.*

**plummy**

(adj.) PLUHM-ee—(of a voice) mellow and resonant
*The radio announcer's plummy voice soothed the listeners.*

**pluvious**

(adj.) PLOO-vee-uhs—relating to steady rainfall
*The pluvious forecast worried the vacationers.*

**pococurante**

(n.) poh-koh-koo-RAN-tee—a person characterized by indifference or nonchalance
*It is useless to argue with a pococurante.*

**poetaster**

(n.) POH-it-as-tur—a poorly skilled poet
*The poetaster continued to write even though critics slammed his work.*

**pogonip**

(n.) PAH-guh-nip—a dense ice fog
*Driving through a pogonip in the Nevada mountains in the winter can be extremely dangerous.*

**polemic**

(adj.) puh-LEM-ik—controversial nature
*The boss's face turned purple during the polemic meeting.*

**politic**

(adj.) POL-ih-tik—shrewd on practical issues; diplomatic

*It is politic to do your research before investing.*

**polyglot**

(adj.) POL-ee-glot—multilingual

*The polyglot traveler would tell us about his trips in the language of the place he visited.*

**polymath**

(n.) POLL-ee-math—a learned intellectual, skilled in many areas

*The polymath's theories heavily influenced a wide variety of intellectual fields.*

**pomaceous**

(adj.) poh-MEY-shuhs—pertaining to the fruit of the apple family

*The painter was obsessed with pomaceous fruit.*

**popinjay**

(n.) POP-in-jay—a conceited and talkative person

*The popinjay's favorite topic of conversation was himself.*

**porcine**

(adj.) PAWR-sayn—relating to or resembling pigs

*His porcine cheeks were stuffed with potato chips.*

**portentous**

(adj.) pawr-TEN-tuhs—momentous in nature; amazing

*Crowds gathered to watch the portentous street performer.*

**postprandial**

(adj.) post-PRAN-dee-ul—occurring after meal

*Due to the bad weather, Larry was unable to go outside to have a postprandial cigarette.*

**postulant**

(n.) POS-chuh-luhnt—an applicant for admission, especially for a religious order
*The postulant was nervous before taking his vows.*

**potentate**

(n.) POHT-n-teyt—a ruler with supreme authority
*No one dared question the potentate's authority.*

**prate**

(v.) PREYT—speaking at length in a foolish manner
*Her in-laws prated through the entire dinner.*

**praxis**

(n.) PRAK-seez—practical application or custom
*Instead of speculating about theories on evolution, Jim chose a praxis method of interviewing many citizens.*

**precatory**

(adj.) PREK-uh-tawr-ee—expressing a wish or prayer
*She refused to listen to their precatory overtures for more money.*

**prelusive**

(adj.) preh-LOO-siv—of a prelude, introductory in nature
*The keynote speaker's prelusive remarks caught the audience's attention.*

**preponderant**

(adj.) preh-PON-der-uhnt—having superseding importance
*Cash flow was the preponderant issue at the company meeting.*

**prepone**

(v.) preh-POHN—to schedule for an earlier time or date
*The meeting on Friday was preponed to Thursday so that the boss could have a long weekend.*

**prestidigitator**

(n.) pres-tih-DIG-ih-tuh-tawr—a magician

*The amateur prestidigitator broke his leg while trying a levitation trick.*

**pretermit**

(v.) pree-ter-MIT—to omit

*He opted to pretermit his fraud conviction in the job interview.*

**prevaricate**

(v.) prih-VAIR-uh-kayt—to stray from or avoid the truth

*Power can easily lead a susceptible leader to prevaricate.*

**priggish**

(adj.) PRIG-ish—self-righteously exact or moralistic

*She told her father to stop being priggish about her life choices.*

**primogeniture**

(n.) pray-moh-JEN-ih-choor—an exclusive right of inheritance belonging to the firstborn son

*Xavier inherited the throne by primogeniture.*

**pro forma**

(adj.) pro-FOR-muh—conducted as a formality, perfunctory

*After the mayor's last rival dropped out, the town had a one-candidate pro forma election.*

**procacity**

(n.) pro-KA-suh-tee—a propensity to display petulance

*The young man's procacity was unbearable.*

**procellous**

(adj.) proh-SEL-uhs—turbulent, tempestuous; as the sea

*Pam's mood matched the procellous weather outside.*

## proclivity

(n.) proh-KLIV-ih-tee—a natural or habitual leaning or tendency

*It was his proclivity to drink two cups of coffee each morning.*

## procryptic

(adj.) proh-KRIP-tik—being a pattern that conceals, often from predators

*The stick insect and leaf frog are both highly procryptic.*

## procumbent

(adj.) proh-KUHM-buhnt—reclining or stretching out face down

*The procumbent beach bum had a sunburned back.*

## profligacy

(n.) PROF-lih-gah-see—wickedly irresponsible, extravagant

*The rock group worked hard to maintain its image of profligacy.*

## progenitor

(n.) proh-JEN-ih-ter—a direct family predecessor or ancestor

*Hank had a long line of progenitors who were carpenters.*

## prognosticate

(v.) prog-NOS-tih-keyt—to forecast or foresee

*The newscaster prognosticated the outcome of the game during the fifth inning.*

## prolix

(adj.) PRO-liks—rambling or flippant

*I could not keep my eyes open as I tried to finish the unbearably prolix book.*

## promissory

(adj.) PROM-miss-or-ee—full of potential

*The movie trailer was promissory of action and adventure, but the film itself was a bore.*

**promulgate**

(v.) PROM-uhl-geyt—to proclaim officially

*Barbara decided she would promulgate her candidacy at the press conference.*

**propinquity**

(n.) proh-PING-kwih-tee—nearness in area; proximity

*The propinquity of the cubicles at work made Craig feel suffocated.*

**propound**

(v.) pruh-POUND—to advise or suggest

*Lisa propounded a radical new strategy for the sales team.*

**proprioception**

(n.) proh-pree-uh-SEP-shun—the ability to discern the posture and movement of one's body

*Gymnasts work hard to develop their proprioception.*

**prorogue**

(v.) proh-ROAG—to halt a session of

*According to law, the nation's leader may prorogue the parliament at any time.*

**prosaic**

(adj.) proh-ZEY-ik—ordinary or dull

*Mainstream radio has a tendency to be overly prosaic.*

What's wrong with being a boring kind of guy?

—**George H. W. Bush**

**prospicience**

(n.) proh-SPI-shens—predict

*Weathermen are not always on target when they try to prospicience the weather.*

**protean**

(adj.) PROH-tee-uhn—highly variable; changing

*His protean personality adapts to any social situation.*

**provenance**

(n.) PROV-uh-nuhnts—location of beginning

*The antiquities were of Egyptian provenance.*

**provender**

(n.) PROV-uhn-duhr—parched food used as farm animal feed

*Farmers use hay as a provender for horses.*

**provenience**

(n.) prov-EEN-yuns—a starting place or origin

*The provenience of the speech was from the Bible.*

**provincialism**

(n.) pro-VIN-shuh-liz-uhm—a narrow-minded or ignorant mind-set

*She was embarrassed by her parents' provincialism.*

**psittacine**

(adj.) SIT-uh-seen—relating to parrots

*The psittacine zoologist often visited the Amazon.*

**pudency**

(n.) PYOOD-n-see—modesty, humbleness

*Bo's pudency hurt him at interviews because it was difficult for him to talk about past accomplishments.*

**puerile**

(adj.) PYOO-uhr-ayl—immature, childish

*Peggy's puerile jokes were not funny at all.*

**puffery**

(n.) PUHF-er-ee—lofty praise

*His biography was loaded with puffery.*

**pugilist**

(n.) PYOO-juh-list—a fist-fighter or boxer

*The pugilist's flattened nose was his badge of honor, representing all the years he spent in the ring.*

**pugnacious**

(adj.) puhg-NEY-shus—combative in conduct; belligerent

*Trisha acquired a pugnacious attitude when she hit thirteen.*

**puisne**

(adj.) PYOO-nay—inferior, subordinate

*The puisne judge was assigned to all the tedious tax trials.*

**puissant**

(adj.) PWIS-unt—forceful, strong, mighty

*The puissant company opened its stores all across the area.*

**pukka**

(adj.) PUHK-uh—genuine

*His grandmother's pukka cuisine was better than any restaurant's.*

**pulchritude**

(n.) PUHL-krih-tood—physical attractiveness

*Sally had a certain type of pulchritude that made men not want to turn away.*

**pule**

(v.) PYOOL—whimper, moan

*"I don't want to hear you pule about overtime work," said the boss.*

**pullulate**

(v.) PUHL-yuh-leyt—sprout, take root

*The greens keeper ensured the grass pullulated perfectly.*

**punctilious**

(adj.) punk-TIL-ee-uss—meticulous
*Writers admired the punctilious editor.*

**purdah**

(n.) PUR-duh—social isolation
*Gina's friends placed her in purdah after they found out she was spreading rumors about them.*

**purl**

(v.) PERL—to flow with rippling movements and a gentle sound
*She watched the stream purl through the ravine.*

**purloin**

(v.) pur-LOYN—to rob
*Needing money, Warren and Nick planned to purloin all they could from the cash register.*

**purview**

(n.) PUR-vyoo—the extent or span of something
*The testimony was beyond the purview of the investigation.*

**pusillanimous**

(adj.) pyoo-suh-LAN-uh-muhs—gutless, lacking courage
*Chris broke up with Courtney in a pusillanimous e-mail.*

> There are several good protections against temptations but the surest is cowardice.
> **—Mark Twain**

**putative**

(adj.) PYOO-tuh-tiv—presumed, alleged

*Tory's daughter was the putative heir to his fortune.*

**putsch**

(n.) POOCH—a sudden attempt by a group, usually political

*Hitler was sent to prison in 1923 after a putsch that he led failed.*

**pyknic**

(adj.) PIK-nik—having a tiny, stocky body type

*The pyknic man was unable to qualify for the marathon.*

# Q

**quadragenarian**

(n.) kwod-ruh-juh-NAIR-ee-uhn—a person who is between forty and forty-nine years old
*Mike felt old the day he became a quadragenarian.*

**quaff**

(n.) KWAF—to chug an alcoholic beverage
*Ralph quaffed the beer in several gulps.*

**quaggy**

(adj.) KWAG-ee—soft or soggy
*A newborn baby's behind is quite quaggy.*

**qualmish**

(adj.) KWAH-mish—prone to questions of morality
*Qualmish Tom always thought twice about his actions.*

**quay**

(n.) KEE—a landing space where ships load and unload
*The opening of the quay along the shoreline helped to create a lot of jobs for the area.*

**quiddity**

(n.) KWID-ih-tee—the authentic essence of a thing that sets it apart
*Only by sampling the succulent peach could Simone experience the true quiddity of the precious fruit.*

**quidnunc**

(n.) KWID-nungk—a gossip
*Every office has its own quidnunc.*

> The only time people dislike gossip is when
> you gossip about them.
>
> **—Will Rogers**

**quiescent**

(adj.) kwee-ES-uhnt—motionless, quiet
*The quiescent phone didn't ring all day.*

**quisling**

(n.) KWIZ-ling—a disloyal conspirator
*The quisling sold the company's secret recipes to its competitors.*

**quitclaim**

(v.) KWIT-klaym—to relinquish claim to
*The divorce court judge ruled that Chris had to quitclaim the house to his wife.*

**quixotic**

(adj.) kwik-SOT-ik—impulsive and irrational
*Gary has taken on the quixotic mission to save the failing company.*

**quondam**

(adj.) KWON-dum—former
*The quondam flower child, who once denounced the business world, grew up to become a CEO.*

# quotidian

(adj.) kwoh-TID-ee-uhn—customary, usual

*John, who was perfectly comfortable with his quotidian life, never sought adventure or change.*

# R

**raconteur**

(n.) rack-on-TUR—a skilled storyteller

*The raconteur could turn any mediocre story into an interesting one.*

**raffish**

(adj.) RAF-ish—gaudily improper or nonconformist

*The raffish young man wooed women with his devil-may-care attitude.*

**raiment**

(n.) RAY-ment—standard attire

*The queen changed into regal raiment for the palace party.*

**rankle**

(v.) RANK-ul—to cause persistent annoyance

*The neighbor's new Mercedes rankles Hank more than he wants to admit.*

**rapacious**

(adj.) ruh-PAY-shuhs—overly greedy, or predatory

*The rapacious police officers were suspended for their actions.*

**rara avis**

(n.) RAIR-uh-AY-vis—characterized by rarity; literally, rare bird

*He was that rara avis—an honest criminal.*

**rathskeller**

(n.) RAHT-skel-er—a bar or restaurant usually below street level

*Every rathskeller they visited was packed like a sardine can.*

> Some people ask the secret of our long marriage. We take time to go to a restaurant two times a week. A little candlelight, dinner, soft music and dancing . . . She goes Tuesdays, I go Fridays.
>
> **—Henry Youngman**

**ratiocination**

(n.) rash-ee-oh-sin-EY-shun—the process of reasoning

*The philosophy society adhered to strict rules of ratiocination.*

**ratiocinative**

(adj.) rash-ee-os-i-NEY-tiv—marked by logic in thought

*Laura was promoted for her ratiocinative ability to solve any company problem.*

**rebarbative**

(adj.) ree-BAHR-buh-tiv—invoking irritation

*The man at the club turned into a rebarbative creep when Wilma wouldn't dance with him.*

**recalcitrant**

(adj.) ree-KAL-sih-trahnt—disobedient to authority

*Her recalcitrant son arrived home late once again.*

**recherché**

(adj.) ruh-sher-SHAY—infrequently found; rare

*The movie buffs talked about recherché films interesting only to them.*

**recidivist**

(n.) rih-SID-uh-vist—one who repeatedly breaks the law

*The recidivist thief received a stiff jail sentence.*

**redolent**

(adj.) RED-uh-luhnt—having a sweet aroma

*The kitchen was redolent of apple crisp and coffee.*

**redoubt**

(n.) reh-DOWT—a refuge or defense

*The troops huddled in a redoubt while they waited for fresh supplies.*

**redoubtable**

(adj.) reh-DOW-tuh-bul—formidable, evoking admiration

*The redoubtable Michael Jordan retired for the last time.*

**redound**

(v.) rih-DOWND—to have a result with a good or bad effect

*The success of the show ultimately redounds to the director.*

**refection**

(n.) rih-FEK-shun—a snack

*He went to the hot-dog stand for a refection.*

**refractory**

(adj.) rih-FRAK-tuh-ree—strongly noncompliant

*The refractory child refused to eat his Brussels sprouts.*

**refulgence**

(n.) rih-FUHL-juhnts—shining

*Her eyes displayed unparalleled refulgence as she received her engagement ring.*

**refulgent**

(adj.) rih-FUHL-jent—emitting an intense light

*The refulgent rays from the sun made Tim thankful that he had a window in his office.*

**regnant**

(adj.) REG-nuhnt—ruling or exercising supremacy

*Their company was the regnant force in the industry.*

**relucent**

(adj.) rih-LOO-suhnt—gleaming or reflecting

*The relucent ring caught the hobbit's eye.*

**remonstrate**

(v.) REH-mon-streyt—to object in dissent

*Finding it useless to remonstrate with his boss, Mark cleaned out his desk and left.*

**remontant**

(adj.) rih-MON-tuhnt—blossoming several times annually

*The remontant roses brightened up the garden once again.*

**remunerate**

(v.) rih-MYOO-nuh-reyt—to compensate for work

*Their services were generously remunerated.*

**remuneration**

(n.) rih-myoo-nuh-REY-shun—monetary compensation for services

*Additional services will require remuneration.*

> If you want to know what God thinks of
> money, just look at the people he gave it to.
>
> —**Dorothy Parker**

**renascent**

(adj.) rih-NAS-uhnt—showing reinvigoration

*The guitarist looked forward to the public's renascent interest in rock music.*

**renitent**

(adj.) rih-NAYT-nt—showing persistent opposition

*The guards subdued the renitent prisoner.*

**reprobate**

(n.) REP-roh-beyt—a wicked person

*Hazel, who married a reprobate, was left to raise three children on her own.*

**restive**

(adj.) RESS-tiv—restless, impatient, or anxious

*The restive concert crowd booed the boring opening act.*

**retrench**

(v.) ree-TRENCH—to curtail or cut back

*After years of expansion, some banks are starting to retrench.*

**revanchism**

(n.) ree-VAN-tchism—policies in support of regaining lost territory

*The mediator urged the warring factions to stop their revanchism.*

**revenant**

(n.) REV-vuh-nunt—ghost

*Revenants roamed wild in the horror movie.*

**rhapsodic**

(adj.) rap-SOD-ik—marked by extreme fervor

*There was nothing but rhapsodic praise for the new musical.*

**rheum**

(n.) ROOM—a mucous discharge during illness

*Andrew kept a box of tissues nearby in case of any possible rheum.*

**rhonchus**

(n.) RONG-kuss—a wheezing sound due to mucous buildup

*The man emitted a huge rhonchus as he fell asleep.*

**ribaldry**

(n.) RIB-ahl-dree—vulgar or mocking speech

*The foreman told his crew to cut out the ribaldries and get to work.*

**rictus**

(n.) RIK-tuhs—an open mouth

*Her mouth sprang open to a rictus of shock as she spied the tiny jewelry box under the tree.*

**rimose**

(adj.) RAY-mohs—cracking

*The forest contained many trees with rimose bark.*

**rimple**

(n.) RIM-puhl—a crinkle or crease

*Ken's shirt had been folded for so long that it was nearly impossible to iron out the rimples.*

**ripsnorter**

(n.) RIP-snor-tur—a extremely strong or violent person or object

*The storm was a real ripsnorter, knocking down trees and power lines.*

**risible**

(adj.) RIZ-uh-bul—having the disposition to laugh

*Gino's attempts at cooking were risible.*

**robustious**

(adj.) roh-BUHS-chuss—loud or raucous

*The bus near the school was always packed with robustious teenagers.*

**rodomontade**

(n.) rod-uh-mon-TEYD—boastful speech

*Her date's unsavory rodomontade spurred Piper to skip dessert and ask for the check.*

**roister**

(v.) ROY-stur—displaying uproarious conduct

*Jerome, who went to parties every night, was the epitome of the roistering college student.*

**roseate**

(adj.) ROH-zee-it—showing blind optimism

*Jim's roseate views were not in touch with reality.*

**roundelay**

(n.) ROUND-uh-lay—a song with a phrase or chorus repeated continually

*The children sang a roundelay on the school bus.*

**roustabout**

(n.) ROUST-uh-bout—an unskilled laborer
*Tim dreamed of ditching college to become a roustabout and travel across the United States.*

**rubicund**

(adj.) ROO-bih-kund—having a reddish tinge
*Her face was rubicund with embarrassment.*

**ruction**

(n.) RUK-shun—an argument or quarrel
*The neighbors' ruction ended without any injuries.*

**ruderal**

(adj.) ROO-der-uhl—(of a plant) the ability to grow in poor land or rubbish
*Ruderal wildflowers lined the highway.*

**ruffian**

(n.) RUHF-ee-ahn—a brutish or lawless person
*The boy was labeled a ruffian by his mother after fighting with his siblings.*

**ruggedized**

(adj.) RUHG-id-ayzd—capable of resisting shock or vibration
*The military computers were ruggedized to withstand the harsh conditions of combat.*

**ruminate**

(v.) ROO-min-eyt—to contemplate or reflect upon
*She liked to take long walks and ruminate about life.*

**runagate**

(n.) RUN-uh-geyt—a vagabond or wanderer
*The usurper's supporters included a small group of runagates.*

# S

**sabulous**

(adj.) SAB-yuh-luhs—having a sandy texture
*I took a shower to get rid of the sabulous feeling that came from a day at the beach.*

**sacerdotal**

(adj.) sas-er-DOHT-l—relating to a priest
*The priest's sacerdotal vestments were embroidered with gold.*

**sagacious**

(adj.) sa-GEY-shus—showing good judgment and practicality
*The librarian who retired a millionaire was sagacious; she never wasted a penny.*

**salmagundi**

(n.) sal-muh-GUHN-dee—a wide assortment, usually pertaining to food
*The party platter consisted of a salmagundi of sandwiches, crackers, and cheese.*

**saltation**

(n.) sawl-TEY-shun—an abrupt hopping movement
*The sprinters warmed up with some saltation before the race.*

**salubrious**

(adj.) sah-LOO-bree-uhs—promoting health
*Sam only ate salubrious foods because he wanted to lose weight.*

**samhainophobia**

(n.) sah-win-oh-FOH-bee-uh—the condition whereby a person fears Halloween

*Sam, who suffers from samhainophobia, refused to go trick-or-treating.*

> On Halloween, the parents sent their kids out looking like me.
>
> **—Rodney Dangerfield**

**sanative**

(adj.) SAN-ah-tiv—bearing healing qualities

*A study proved the sanative powers of the medication.*

**sang-froid**

(n.) SANG-frwah—composure in the face of adversity

*Gavin showed great sang-froid by quickly administering CPR on the little girl.*

**sanguine**

(adj.) SANG-gwin—showing hope or cheer

*Sherry's sanguine attitude annoys her co-workers on dreary Monday mornings.*

**sanguineous**

(adj.) sang-GWIN-ee-uhs—relating to or containing blood

*Sanguineous movies make me queasy.*

**sapid**

(adj.) SAY-pid—flavorful, or pleasing to taste

*The sapid nectarine was refreshing after a day at the beach.*

**sapient**

(adj.) SAY-pee-unt—having great intelligence or judgment
*In a perfect world leaders would be sapient.*

> I once said cynically of a politician, "He'll double-cross that bridge when he comes to it."
>
> **—Oscar Levant**

**sardonic**

(adj.) sar-DON-ik—angrily derisive or skeptical
*He had a sardonic grin on his face as he listened to his manager's ridiculous proposal.*

**sartorial**

(adj.) sar-TOR-ee-uhl—of or relating to clothing styles produced by tailors
*The actress was lauded by the magazines for her sartorial style.*

**saturnalian**

(adj.) sah-ter-NAY-lee-an—uninhibited in revelry
*His saturnalian friend was the life of the party.*

**saturnine**

(adj.) SAT-er-nayn—of a depressing nature
*The rock star remained saturnine despite becoming a multimillionaire.*

**scabrous**

(adj.) SKA-bruss—having a rough exterior
*The lizard has scabrous skin, but is nonetheless enjoyable to pet.*

**scapegrace**

(n.) SKAYP-grayss—an unscrupulous or rogue person
*Jan's youngest brother, being a scapegrace, humiliated his entire family.*

**scaramouch**

(n.) skair-uh-MOOSH—a mischievous person; scalawag
*The author was a scaramouch with a pen, hiding behind his nom de plume.*

**schadenfreude**

(n.) SHAHD-n-froy-duh—gratification in misfortunes of others
*Since he was next in line to be manager, Gary felt schadenfreude when his boss was fired.*

**schlock**

(adj.) SHLOK—of poor or cheap quality; garbage
*The roof leaked when it rained because it was made of schlock material.*

**scintilla**

(n.) sin-TIL-uh—a small trace
*Hope had a scintilla of doubt when she uttered the words, "I do."*

**sciolism**

(n.) SAY-uh-liz-uhm—shallow or phony knowledge
*Jerry Springer seems to engage in sciolism on his talk show.*

**scrag**

(n.) SKRAG—a skinny person or animal
*The scrag was so skinny that even a medium-size shirt was too loose for him to wear.*

**scrofulous**

(adj.) SKRAW-fyoo-luss—marked by corruption
*The scrofulous border guard accepted the bribe.*

**scurrilous**

(adj.) SKUH-ril-uss—offensive or insulting

*He was offended by her scurrilous remarks.*

**scuttlebutt**

(n.) SKUT-l-but—a water fountain on a vessel

*There was a scuttlebutt in each hallway on the cruise for parched passengers.*

**seditious**

(adj.) seh-DISH-uss—promoting rebellion or discontent with a government

*The government was not amused by the activist's seditious speech.*

**sempiternal**

(adj.) sem-pih-TUR-nl—endless; eternal

*The river's sempiternal flow was soothing to hear.*

**senectitude**

(n.) sih-NEK-tih-tood—the elderly stage of life

*John felt, after eighty years, that he was now entering into a period of senectitude.*

> When I was young I was called a rugged individualist. When I was in my fifties I was considered eccentric. Here I am doing and saying the same things I did then and I'm labeled senile.
>
> —**George Burns**

**senescence**

(n.) sih-NEH-sunhnts—characterized by old age

*Fred's body, impacted by senescence, took a long time to recover from the injury.*

**sententious**

(adj.) sen-TEN-shus—self-righteous

*Joe was sententious as he tried to impress his boss.*

**sentient**

(adj.) SEN-shee-uhnt—capable of perception

*Scientists continue to search for evidence that there are sentient beings outside of Earth.*

**sepulture**

(n.) SEP-uhl-cher—the act of formal burial; as in a tomb

*The sepulture took place at dusk.*

**sere**

(adj.) SEER—dried out, parched

*The rain helped relieve the sere landscape.*

**seriatim**

(adv.) seer-i-EY-tim—succeeding one by one

*The students lined up for a photo seriatim by height.*

**serried**

(adj.) SEYR-eed—crammed together, as troops in formation

*A serried row of trees kept intruders off the property.*

**sesquipedalian**

(adj.) ses-kwuh-puh-DEYL-yuhn—characterized by using complex words

*The speaker was so sesquipedalian that no one understood him.*

**shalloon**

    (n.) SHAH-loon—a weightless woolen fabric used most often for coat linings

    *While searching through the attic, Brenda found a coat with a tattered shalloon.*

**shibboleth**

    (n.) SHIB-uh-lith—a word or pronunciation differentiating one people from another

    *To enter the secret meeting, one would need to know the group's shibboleth.*

**siccative**

    (adj.) SIK-ah-tiv—bringing about the absorption of water

    *The siccative crackers made him thirsty.*

**sidereal**

    (adj.) say-DEER-ee-uhl—relating to or determined by the stars

    *A sidereal day is about four minutes shorter than a solar day.*

**simon-pure**

    (adj.) SAY-mun-pyur—legitimately pure; genuine

    *Growing up in Boston made Janet a simon-pure Red Sox fan.*

**simper**

    (v.) SYM-per—to grin in a silly, coy way

    *His simper led the coach to command, "Wipe that smile off your face, son."*

**simulacrum**

    (n.) sim-yuh-LAY-kruhm—a likeness or depiction

    *After the illness, Marty was a pale simulacrum of the man he used to be.*

**sine die**

(adv.) SAY-nuh day-ee—without agreeing on a time for a future meeting
*The council was adjourned sine die.*

**sine qua non**

(n.) sin-ih kwah NON—a necessary component
*A cake is a sine qua non of any child's birthday party.*

**sinecure**

(n.) SAY-nih-kyorr—a job that requires little work, especially one that is very profitable
*Critics viewed the retired executive's function on the board as a sinecure.*

**sinews**

(n.) SIN-yooz—something supplying strength or power
*People are the sinews of any organization.*

**sinistromanual**

(adj.) sin-ih-stro-MAN-yoo-ul—having a dominant left hand or foot
*The sinistromanual student would get ink stains on the side of his hand when writing with pen.*

**Sisyphean**

(adj.) siss-ih-FEE-an—never-ending
*Harris had the Sisyphean task of trying to keep his house clean.*

**sitzmark**

(n.) SITS-mahrk—an indentation in the snow made by a backward-falling skier
*The inexperienced skier left sitzmarks all over the mountain.*

**skein**

(n.) SKEYN—a coiled bundle of yarn
*The cat liked to play with the skein.*

**skewbald**

(adj.) SKEEOO-bald—being colored with patches of brown and white
*The skewbald horse won the race.*

**skinflint**

(n.) SKIN-flint—a mean or parsimonious person
*The skinflint would steal napkins from the diner so he wouldn't have to buy them at the store.*

> I won't say he's cheap but he can squeeze a nickel so hard the _e pluribus_ hangs over the _unum_.
>
> —**Bob Hope**

**slake**

(v.) SLEYK—to alleviate or satisfy
*The white wine slaked her thirst, helping to wash down the turkey.*

**slapdash**

(adj.) SLAP-dash—in a hurried, careless manner
*Sarah's slapdash nature did not help her chances of becoming a news editor.*

**slovenly**

(adj.) SLUV-un-lee—messy or disorderly in appearance
*Many people were not let into the nightclub because of their slovenly apparel.*

**slugabed**

(n.) SLUHG-ah-bed—one whose laziness prevents them from getting out of bed on time

*I notice Gregory up before me as usual, for I am a sad slugabed.*

**smaragdine**

(adj.) smuh-RAG-deen—pertaining to emeralds

*Ireland is historically known as a smaragdine island.*

**snickersnee**

(n.) SNIK-ur-snee—a large, sharp blade used as a weapon

*The pirate would use a snickersnee during combat.*

**sobriquet**

(n.) SO-bree-kay—a moniker or alias

*At work, his sobriquet was "Flash" because he finished assignments so fast.*

**soi-disant**

(adj.) swah dee-ZAHN—labeling oneself thus; pretending to be

*The soi-disant consultant had no degree of any kind.*

**soigné**

(adj.) swan-YAY—done or designed in an elegant manner

*The soigné tennis player signed autographs for over an hour after his match.*

**somnambulant**

(adj.) som-NAM-byoo-lent—of walking or performing tasks during sleep

*Todd's somnambulant state during class aggravated his teachers.*

**somnifacient**

(adj.) som-nuh-FAY-shunt—producing or causing slumber

*Harry always felt lazy after taking the somnifacient pills.*

**somniferous**

(adj.) sawm-NIF-er-uss—inducing sleep with outside influence
*The five-hundred-page report was somniferous.*

**somniloquy**

(n.) som-NIL-uh-kwee—the act of sleep talking
*Nick's somniloquy was a reflection of his uneasy mind.*

**somnolence**

(n.) SOM-nuh-luns—state of lethargy or drowsiness
*The lack of ventilation in the office caused the employee's somnolence.*

**soporific**

(adj.) so-po-RIH-fik—causing or pertaining to sleep
*The critic said the movie was soporific and gave it a poor review.*

**soubise**

(n.) soo-BEEZ—a sauce made with prepared onions and containing meat
*The onion farmer loved to cover all of his dinner meals with soubise.*

**sough**

(v.) SOW—to make a gentle, rustling sound
*The trees soughed in the soft summer breeze.*

**soupçon**

(n.) soop-SON—a tiny quantity, a remnant
*Mark refused to show even a soupçon of mercy to the fly that was buzzing around the house.*

**spatchcock**

(v.) SPATCH-kawk—to split and prepare a fowl for grilling
*His grandmother spatchcocked the turkey so dinner would be ready on time.*

**speciesism**

(n.) SPEE-shee-ziz-uhm—discrimination of other species usually by humans

*Some animal rights activists argue that speciesism is a type of prejudice.*

**spelunker**

(n.) speh-LUHNG-ker—one that hikes and searches caves

*The experienced spelunker was trapped in a cave-in.*

**spindrift**

(n.) SPIN-drift—ocean spray that becomes airborne due to wind

*Heavy spindrift made it difficult for the captain to chart the course.*

**spoony**

(adj.) SPOO-nee—excessively emotional or sappy

*The spoony relationship gave way to such bitter fighting.*

**sprightly**

(adj.) SPRAYT-lee—brimming with vigor and vivacity

*The sprightly band made the party one to remember.*

**spumescent**

(adj.) spyoo-MES-uhnt—frothy

*The spumescent latte was thick and creamy.*

**squinch**

(v.) SKWINTCH—to contort or warp one's facial features

*She squinched her eyes shut during most of the horror movie.*

**stagflation**

(n.) stag-FLAY-shun—a period of broad economic stagnation

*The country's stagflation worried the economists.*

**stanch**

(v.) STONCH—to obstruct the flow of

*Allen used a mop to stanch the water flowing into the kitchen.*

**stegophilist**

(n.) steg-of-IL-ist—one who scales the outside of skyscrapers for sport

*The stegophilist had trouble obtaining an insurance policy.*

**stentorian**

(adj.) sten-TOR-ee-an—deafening

*They were awoken by a stentorian crack of thunder.*

**sternutation**

(n.) stur-nyoo-TAY-shun—sneezing

*Quentin has long bouts of sternutation whenever he is in a dusty area.*

**sternutatory**

(adj.) ster-NYO-tah-tor-ee—being the cause of sneezing

*Pepper is a sternutatory substance.*

**stertorous**

(adj.) STUR-tuh-ruhs—snoring

*Leonard's breathing was so stertorous that it was impossible to sleep in his presence.*

**sthenic**

(adj.) STHEN-ik—robust, vigorous, physically built

*Alex became sthenic by spending long hours at the gym listening to Madonna.*

**stochastic**

(adj.) stuh-KAS-tik—of a randomly determined sequence

*Maura's stochastic nature keeps her co-workers on their toes.*

## stolid

(adj.) STAHL-id—lacking emotion
*The stolid professor put the class to sleep.*

## stricture

(n.) STRIKT-yer—a regulation or constraint
*The dictator imposed tough strictures on the country's citizens.*

## stultify

(v.) STUL-tuh-fy—to make one appear to be idiotic or stupid
*The tenured teacher was never reprimanded despite being known to stultify students.*

> Those who can, do. Those that can't, teach. Those who can't teach, teach gym. Those who can't teach gym become presidents.
>
> **—Woody Allen**

## subaltern

(adj.) sub-AWL-tern—lower in status
*Jamie was able to climb the corporate ladder by never forgetting her subaltern days.*

## subfusc

(adj.) sub-FUHSK—dreary
*Politicians intentionally make their endeavors seem subfusc so that there will be less opposition to their policies.*

## subitaneous

(adj.) sub-ih-TEY-ne-ous—abrupt; hastily done
*Sam's subitaneous lunch consisted of a pickle, blueberry yogurt, and some Cheez-Its.*

**subrogate**

(v.) SUB-roh-geyt—to substitute or replace one for another
*Dan Aykroyd and Eddie Murphy were subrogated by a cruel bet in* Trading Places.

**subsume**

(v.) sub-SOOM—to consider or incorporate as a part of a larger group
*The soprano's voice was subsumed by the orchestral arrangement.*

**subterfuge**

(n.) SUB-tur-fyooj—a device or strategy used to conceal or evade something
*Sally used subterfuge to trick Mike into proposing to her, pretending to be a sweet girl.*

**succedaneum**

(n.) suhk-sih-DEY-nee-uhm—a replacement
*Rice cakes are not the best succedaneum for chips.*

**succor**

(v.) SUHK-or—to help or aid
*She managed to succor the man before he fell over.*

**sudatorium**

(n.) soo-duh-TAWR-ee-um—a hot room meant to cause perspiration; sauna
*The sudatorium was the place where the workers could relax after a workout.*

**sui generis**

(adj.) soo-aye JEN-ur-us—distinctive; uncommon
*Rebecca's bizarre personality showed that she was sui generis.*

**sumpter**

(n.) SUMP-ter—an animal such as a mule used to transport goods
*We loaded up the sumpter before we hit the trail.*

**sunder**

(v.) SUN-der—to separate or split up
*Civil war threatened to sunder the nation.*

**superannuated**

(adj.) soo-pur-AN-yoo-ey-tid—obsolete due to age; outmoded
*The company's superannuated dress code required women to wear skirts.*

**supererogatory**

(adj.) soop-er-ih-ROG-ah-tor-ee—doing more than what is necessary
*The workaholic stayed late to create some new supererogatory projects.*

**supernumerary**

(n.) soo-per-NOO-mer-eyr-ee—an extra component on top of the needed amount
*The hockey team traded its supernumeraries in the draft.*

**supine**

(adj.) soo-PAYN—lying face up on a surface
*He lay supine on the couch, resting after a long day at work.*

**supplicate**

(v.) SUP-lih-kayt—to plead humbly
*The criminal supplicated for forgiveness from his victim.*

**supramundane**

(adj.) su-pra-MUN-dane—positioned above the ground; celestial

*Sarah wished she had supramundane powers to stop time so that she wouldn't be late.*

**suspire**

(v.) suh-SPAYR—to exalt noisily

*Sara swapped the tooth under the pillow for a dollar, suspiring with relief when her son didn't wake up.*

**susurrus**

(n.) su-SUHR-uhs—a delicate whisper

*The countryside had a calming effect on Olivia due in part to the soft susurrus of the autumn breeze.*

**sybarite**

(n.) SIB-uh-rayt—one who is dedicated to lavishness and pleasure

*The sybarite would only eat the finest French cuisine.*

**sycophant**

(n.) SIK-ah-fant—an exorbitant flatterer

*With his eagerness to please, the new hire quickly became known as the office sycophant.*

**sylph**

(n.) SILF—a slim, elegant woman; someone fairylike

*The sylph's ballet performance was poetry in motion.*

**sylvan**

(adj.) SIL-van—pertaining to the forest or wooded area

*The guys became one with nature on their sylvan retreat.*

# T

**tabescent**

(adj.) tuh-BES-unt—becoming increasingly emaciated
*The shipwrecked explorer lay on the island in a tabescent state.*

**taciturn**

(adj.) TAS-i-turn—overly reserved
*There was something soothing about Willow's taciturn personality.*

**tantamount**

(adj.) TAN-tuh-mount—equal in effect of significance
*Jen singing was tantamount to torture.*

**tarantism**

(n.) TAR-un-tiz-um—an uncontainable desire to dance
*Some Italians in the seventeenth-century thought tarantism was
   caused by the bite of a tarantula.*

**tarradiddle**

(n.) tair-uh-DID-uhl—an insignificant fib; an untruth
*Tarradiddles are not worth the trouble they cause.*

**tarsalgia**

(n.) tahr-SAL-jea—an ache in the foot
*The adorable shoes gave Sharon a terrible tarsalgia.*

**tatterdemalion**

(adj.) ta-ter-de-MEYL-ee-un—a person in shabby clothes
*"When did casual Friday become tatterdemalion Friday?" the boss
   asked.*

**tautology**

(n.) taw-TOL-oh-jee—pointless repetition of an idea using different wording
*The editors said the article was riddled with tautology.*

**telic**

(adj.) TEL-ik—aimed at an objective, purpose
*Andrew's telic nature would not let him fail in any of his endeavors.*

**temerarious**

(adj.) tem-er-AIR-ee-uss—uncontrollable or rash
*It would have been temerarious not to check the mirror before merging into the highway.*

**temerity**

(n.) tuh-MER-uh-tee—strong disregard for danger
*The driver of the SUV had the temerity to accelerate out of every icy turn.*

**tenebrous**

(adj.) TEN-uh-bruss—melancholy; depressing
*The castle halls were tenebrous.*

**tergiversate**

(v.) TER-gih-ver-seyt—making inconsistent statements with respect to a topic
*The investigators warned the suspect not to tergiversate.*

**termagant**

(n.) TUR-ma-gant—a brutal, bullying woman
*Jane was known as a termagant, for barking orders at workers.*

**terpsichorean**

(adj.) turp-si-koh-REE-uhn—relating to dance
*The guests, with their terpsichorean activities, were exhausted by midnight.*

**tetchy**

(adj.) TETSH-ee—easily annoyed; ill-tempered

Frank's tetchy personality made him unapproachable.

**tête-à-tête**

(adj.) TEYT-uh-TEYT—a private discussion, usually between two individuals

*With their kids in college, the husband and wife had many tête-à-tête dinners.*

**thaumaturgy**

(n.) THAW-muh-tuhr-jee—a routine focusing on magic

*Most thaumaturgy in film comes to fruition through special effects.*

**threnody**

(n.) THREN-uh-dee—a poem or song of sullen remembrance

*The husband recited his threnody during the eulogy of his wife.*

**tiglon**

(n.) TAY-gluhn—the offspring of a female lion and a male tiger

*Since one of Dan's kids loved lions and the other loved tigers, he took them to see the tiglon at the zoo.*

**tin-pot**

(adj.) TIN-pot—substandard; mediocre

*The tin-pot baseball field was overgrown with weeds.*

**tincture**

(n.) TINGK-cher—a smidgen

*I detected a faint tincture of disapproval in my mother's voice.*

**tintinnabulation**

(n.) tin-tih-nab-yuh-LAY-shuhn—a ringing sound; usually of bells

*The tintinnabulations of the cymbals that echoed during the concert put Manny in a trance.*

**titivate**

(v.) TIT-uh-veyt—to tidy up; improve the appearance of

*The old farmer titivated his outfit for his date by sporting a new pair of dungarees.*

**tittle-tattle**

(n.) TIT-uhl TAT-uhl—excessive chatter; gossip

*Jimmy would give anything for the girls to stop their tittle-tattle in class.*

**tmesis**

(n.) tuh-MEE-sys—the insertion of one word in the middle of another

*Caleb used tmesis to describe his favorite baseball player as un-freaking-believable!*

**toady**

(n.) TOH-dee—an annoying flatterer

*Her co-worker was a toady to the boss.*

> I don't want any yes-men around me. I want everybody to tell me the truth even if it costs them their jobs.
>
> —**Samuel Goldwyn**

**tocsin**

(n.) TOK-sin—the loud sound of an alarm or signal

*The flood was a tocsin to the dangers of global warming.*

**toilsome**

(adj.) TOY'L-sum—of intense labor

*They ate a hearty dinner after the toilsome mountain trek.*

**tonsure**

(n.) TON-sher—the act of shaving all one's hair off

*Tonsure is a part of becoming a monk.*

**toper**

(n.) TOH-puhr—a serious alcoholic

*The toper becomes very belligerent whenever he drinks.*

**torpid**

(adj.) TAWR-pid—lethargic or slow-moving

*The economists hoped for a turnaround in the torpid economy.*

**toxophilite**

(n.) tok-SOF-ih-layt—a committed archer

*Robin Hood and his men were all toxophilites.*

**traduce**

(v.) trah-DOOS—to slander someone

*The cutthroat co-worker traduced Dean's name around the office in an effort to get the promotion.*

**traipse**

(v.) treyps—to stroll aimlessly about

*Vernon traipsed through the city streets, looking for any sort of employment.*

**tralatitious**

(adj.) trah-lah-TIH-shuss—having been handed down

*The common values of the society were tralatitious.*

**trammel**

(n.) TRAM-uhl—an obstruction to freedom

*In her dreams—free from the trammels of reality—anything could happen.*

**transpontine**

(adj.) trans-PON-tin—located on the other side of a bridge

*Hank was afraid to cross the old rickety bridge and refused to go to the transpontine restaurant.*

**treacly**

(adj.) TREE-klee—overly sweet or sentimental

*The children's books were filled with many treacly stories.*

**trenchant**

(adj.) TREN-chunt—sharply witty

*Troy addressed his wife with trenchant wit during the divorce.*

**trencherman**

(n.) TREN-chuhr-muhn—one with a big appetite; a heavy eater

*The winner of the hot dog–eating contest seemed to be the most dedicated trencherman.*

**trice**

(n.) TRYSS—an extremely brief amount of time, a moment

*Mary is such an efficient worker that it seems like she completes every project in a trice.*

**trig**

(adj.) TRIG—well-kept, as in appearance

*The trig man would always wear a dark suit, light tie, and finely pressed shirt to his interviews.*

**triskaidekaphobia**

(n.) tris-kay-dek-uh-FOH-bee-uh—an extreme fear of the number 13

*Unlike some people who just think the number 13 is bad luck, I have severe triskaidekaphobia.*

**triturate**

(v.) TRICH-uh-rayt—to crush into fine particles

*Naima triturated the crackers with a small spoon to use in her soup.*

**troglodyte**

(n.) TRAWG-loh-dayt—a primal caveman or hermit

*In our cubicles, our behavior resembles that of troglodytes.*

**trophic**

(adj.) TROW-fik—having to do with nutrition

*The food chain is based up trophic dynamics.*

**troublous**

(adj.) TRUHB-luss—characterized by turbulence

*The troublous rioters charged the barricade.*

**truckle**

(v.) TRUCK-uhl—to act in a subordinate way

*Tom refused to truckle to his boss just to get promoted.*

**truculent**

(adj.) TRUHK-yuh-luhnt—extremely brutal; scathing

*During the divorce, bitter and truculent thoughts bombarded my mind.*

**trumpery**

(n.) TRUM-puh-ree—something with no value

*Andrew's desk is stuffed with such trumpery.*

**truncate**

(v.) TRUHNG-keyt—to cut something shorter
*The electrician truncated the tree branch because it was hitting the power line.*

**tucket**

(n.) TUHK-it—a grandiose display
*The visiting dignitaries were greeted by a big tucket.*

**tumefaction**

(n.) too-muh-FAK-shuhn—the act of bulging or ballooning
*Tumefaction occurs within the bodies of blowfish.*

**tumid**

(adj.) TOO-mid—characteristic of swelling
*Ken was taken to the hospital with a tumid leg.*

**turbid**

(adj.) TUR-bid—unclear or blurred; lacking transparency
*The turbid haze in Hazel's head cleared after an hour of yoga.*

**turgid**

(adj.) TUR-jid—pompous in style or language; haughty
*The halls echoed with the turgid rhetoric of the young politician.*

**turophile**

(n.) TOOR-uh-fyle—one who loves cheese
*The new deli, with its five hundred varieties of cheese, is a turophile's heaven.*

How can you be expected to govern a country that has 246 kinds of cheese?

—**Charles de Gaulle**

**turpitude**

(n.) TUR-puh-tood—inherently evil moral makeup

*The businessman was convicted of a crime involving moral turpitude.*

**tutelage**

(n.) TOOT-l-ahj—guidance

*Under the manager's tutelage, the new employee learned the system quickly.*

**tyro**

(n.) TAY-roh—a novice or trainee

*For the tyro rider, being thrown from a horse is a rite of passage.*

# U

**ugsome**

(adj.) UHG-sum—despicable

*The ugsome villain's plans were thwarted by the hero.*

**ukase**

(n.) yoo-KAYS—a definitive command or edict

*My mother's ukase demanded that everyone wash their own dishes.*

**ultraism**

(n.) UHL-tra-izm—an extremist set of ideals

*The activist was prone to ultraism in politics, religion and diet.*

**ultroneous**

(adj.) ul-TRO-nee-ous—spur-of-the-moment

*She said no to his ultroneous proposal.*

**ululate**

(v.) UL-yuh-layt—to howl or holler loudly

*The entire downtown area seemed to ululate during the rally.*

**umbrageous**

(adj.) um-BRAH-juss—likely to be offended

*No one dared make a joke around the umbrageous receptionist.*

**unblenched**

(adj.) un-BLENCHT—unaffected, undaunted

*The unblenched soldiers fought the battle to the best of their abilities.*

## upbraid

(v.) up-BREYD—to scold or uncover fault in

*The residents upbraided the politician for the lack of progress in cleaning up the city.*

## ursprache

(n.) OOR-shprah-khuh—an ancestor of current languages

*Both English and German come from the Indo-European ursprache.*

V

**vacillation**

(n.) vas-uh-LEY-shuhn—a state of indecision or inaction
*His vacillation between majors kept Kevin in college for
    six years.*

**vacuity**

(n.) vuh-KYOO-ih-tee—vacancy, absence
*There was a certain vacuity inside Marvin after his favorite
    team lost in the playoffs.*

**vacuous**

(adj.) VAK-yoo-uhs—displaying a lack of ideas or content
*The vacuous employees failed to come up with a unique proposal.*

**vade mecum**

(n.) vah-dey-MEE-kuhm—a regularly used reference material
*A thesaurus is a must-have vade mecum for writers.*

**vagary**

(n.) vey-GA-ree—an unpredictable act, event or idea
*The babysitter was frustrated by the child's vagaries.*

**valetudinarian**

(adj.) val-ih-tood-in-AIR-ee-an—a sick person who needs to be
cared for
*Winston Churchill was among the most valetudinarian of the
    world's great statesmen.*

## vanguard

(n.) VAN-gard—the leader in a movement; at the forefront
*Music buffs said Pearl Jam was at the vanguard of the grunge music scene.*

## vapid

(adj.) VAP-id—lacking flavor; insipid
*Mom's vapid meatloaf was like a large log of beef.*

## variegate

(v.) VAR-ih-eh-gate—to alter the appearance of something
*Tim variegated the newsletter every month to keep it visually interesting.*

## varlet

(n.) VAHR-lit—an attendant or helper
*He had many varlets at his beck and call.*

## vatic

(adj.) VAT-ik—characteristic of a psychic
*Leonard was so full of himself that he believed that all of his poetry contained vatic messages.*

## vaticinate

(v.) vah-TISS-in-eyt—to predict the future
*The soothsayer vaticinated an end to war.*

## vaunt

(v.) VAWNT—to boast or brag
*Peyton was a star quarterback and used to vaunt his achievements to women, but then broke both his knees.*

## velleity

(n.) veh-LEY-ih-tee—a small, wishful decision
*Lisa had a velleity to start an art collection.*

**venal**

(adj.) VEN-al—susceptible to corruption

*The venal cop didn't give me a ticket after I slipped him a crisp fifty-dollar bill.*

> Power does not corrupt men. Fools, however, if they get into a position of power, corrupt power.
>
> —**George Bernard Shaw**

**venial**

(adj.) VEE-nee-uhl—easily forgiven or excused

*The venial mistake could not stand in the way of their friendship.*

**verdant**

(adj.) VER-dnt—lushly vegetated

*Leonard religiously watered his verdant lawn.*

**veridical**

(adj.) ver-ID-ik-ul—factual, genuine

*He assured the judge his statement was veridical.*

**verily**

(adv.) VER-uh-lee—truly; actually

*I verily believe white shoes should not be worn before Memorial Day.*

## verisimilitude

(n.) ver-uh-si-MIL-ih-tood—the semblance of truth

*The amateur actor fumbled his lines, ruining the play's verisimilitude.*

## verjuice

(n.) VER-joos—the sour liquor of crab apples or unripe grapes

*Sheri was sick of seasoning her salad with oil and vinegar, so she bought a bottle of verjuice dressings.*

## vestigially

(adv.) ves-TIDJ-ah-lee—a trace or small amount

*A strip of tape clung vestigially to one flap of the carton.*

## vexillologist

(n.) vek-suh-LOL-uh-jist—a scholar of flags

*Every vexillologist should know that the thirteen stripes on the American flag symbolize the original colonies.*

## viand

(n.) VEE-ahnd—a tasty, delicious meal

*Sam prepared a savory viand for his wife on their anniversary.*

## vicissitude

(n.) viss-ISS-ih-tood—a variation in the state of things

*Life is full of vicissitudes; you never know where you'll end up.*

## victual

(n.) VIT-l—food provisions intended for humans

*The growing kids ate any victual that was put in front of them.*

## vilipend

(v.) VIL-uh-pend—to vilify or treat with hatred

*Vicky's attempts to vilipend her co-workers made her the office outcast.*

**vim**

(n.) vim—energetic spirit; vitality

*Larry was so full of vim every day that I wondered how many vitamins he was taking.*

**vinaceous**

(adj.) vin-EY-shuss—of red wine's color or texture

*The vinaceous blackberry juice could have been mistaken for a fine Bordeaux wine.*

**virago**

(n.) vee-RAH-goh—a woman of the utmost valor, might, and bravery

*The new CEO, a hardworking virago, turned the struggling start-up into a flourishing firm.*

**virga**

(n.) VER-guh—water and ice particles that evaporate before reaching the ground

*Virga is common in desert areas.*

**virgule**

(n.) VER-gyool—a slash mark used to separate words

*The virgule in* miles/hour *represents the word* per.

**virtu**

(n.) ver-TOO—knowledge of the fine arts

*The host's virtu was evidenced by his large collection of paintings.*

**vitiate**

(v.) VISH-ee-eyt—to reduce the effectiveness of

*His argument was vitiated by factual errors.*

**vitrine**

(n.) vee-TREEN—a glass case used for display

*The actress showcased her awards in a vitrine in her living room.*

**vituperate**

(v.) vih-TOO-per-AT—to criticize with abusive language
*Vicky vituperated her husband when he came home late from work with lipstick on his cheek.*

**vivisepulture**

(n.) viv-uh-SEP-uhl-cher—an act of burying a living person
*My worst nightmare is to be a victim of vivisepulture.*

**vociferous**

(adj.) voh-SIF-uhr-uhs—raucous; loud
*The vociferous kids were fueled by Twinkies and Ding Dongs.*

**volant**

(adj.) VO-lunt—having the ability to fly
*The piece of paper became volant when it was folded into an airplane.*

**volte-face**

(n.) vuhl-tay-FAYSS—a turnaround in strategy or attitude
*The politician did a volte-face after polls showed his position was unpopular.*

**voluble**

(adj.) VOL-yoo-ble—glib, extroverted
*Mary was voluble and always told detailed stories to her friends.*

**voluptuary**

(n.) vuh-LUHP-choo-er-ee—one that devotes their life to extravagance and pleasure
*Victoria, an unabashed voluptuary, enjoyed antique Persian rugs, fur coats, and fine wines.*

**vortiginous**

(adj.) vor-TID-jin-uhs—bearing resemblance to a vortex, spinning

*The Turkish folk dancers spun in a series of vortiginous circles.*

**vulnerary**

(adj.) VUL-nuh-rair-ee—applied in the healing of abrasions

*The herbalist knew everything about vulnerary plants.*

# W

**wamble**

(v.) WOM-bul—(of the stomach) to growl irritably
*Is that your stomach wambling?*

**wan**

(adj.) WAHN—appearing fatigued or unhealthy
*Kevin's wan skin resulted from the disease.*

**warble**

(v.) WOR-bul—to whistle or sing melodiously; to yodel
*Mary woke each morning to the sound of birds warbling outside her window.*

**wastrel**

(n.) WEY-strul—a wasteful person
*Monica was a wastrel at the mall because she knew her parents would pay her credit card bills.*

**waylay**

(v.) WAY-ley—to intercept, usually to rob or seize
*The beggar's goal was to waylay tourists because they seemed to be the kindest.*

**welter**

(n.) WEL-tuhr—a state of commotion or confused mass
*There is a welter of magazines and newspapers strewn about on the table.*

**wen**

(n.) WEHN—a benign cyst or tumor

*As Nathan's hair began to thin, he noticed a wen on his scalp.*

**wheedle**

(v.) WEE-dul—to coerce by flattering persuasion

*She wheedled her way past the bouncer into the nightclub.*

**winsome**

(adj.) WIN-sum—sweetly charming

*Only the winsome were invited to the party.*

**wisenheimer**

(n.) WAY-zen-hay-mer—an arrogant smart aleck

*The wisenheimer was cut down to size by the humble genius.*

**witzelsucht**

(n.) VITS-uhl-sookt—excessive sarcasm and distasteful humor

*Submitting this word might have been a witzelsucht, but I thought it was a good one!*

**wizen**

(v.) WAY-zen—to wilt or become dry

*Sally's plant wizened after she left it on the heater.*

**woolgathering**

(n.) WOOL-gath-uh-ring—indulgence in leisurely daydreaming

*Wendy abandoned her work for woolgathering while staring at her computer screen.*

**wrest**

(v.) rest—to jerk or twist violently

*She wrested her stolen pocketbook from the mugger.*

## xanthosis

(n.) zan-tho-sis—an abnormal golden discoloration of the skin
*Too much carrot juice can cause xanthosis.*

## xeric

(adj.) ZEER-ik—pertaining to a dehydrated environment
*Xeric animals have the ability to survive water shortages.*

## xerophagy

(n.) zih-ROF-uh-jee—the strictest fast in the Eastern Church during Lent
*Some Christians practice xerophagy during Lent.*

**yawp**

(n.) YAWP—a howl, or shout

*The basketball player would always let out a loud yawp whenever he made a slam dunk.*

**yegg**

(n.) YEG—a thug or ruffian

*There's a yegg in this office who steals all the office supplies.*

# Z

## zaftig

(adj.) ZAHF-tig—having a full-bodied, plump figure
*The painter preferred his subjects to be zaftig beauties.*

> I found there was only one way to look thin:
> hang out with fat people.
>
> **—Rodney Dangerfield**

## zomotherapy

(n.) zo-mo-THER-ah-pee—the treatment of disease with intake
of uncooked meat
*Some European physicians claim zomotherapy successfully treats
anemia, debility, and tuberculosis.*

## zoonosis

(n.) zoo-NO-sis—an animal disease that can be transmitted
to humans
*She refused to visit the farm for fear of contracting a zoonosis.*

## zugzwang

(n.) TSOOK-tsvahng—a situation during a chess game in
which a player is forced into a bad move
*I always get stuck in a zugzwang when I play chess with
my father.*

**zumbooruk**

(n.) zum-BOO-ruk—an artillery gun mounted on a camel
*The scholar seemed to choose the most random book at the library: one about the origin of a zumbooruk.*

**zwieback**

(n.) TSVEE-bak—a dry-toasted, egg-rich bread
*Mom's homemade zwiebacks are delicious with a cup of tea.*

A book is a gift you can open again
and again.

—Garrison Keillor

The day after tomorrow is the third day of
the rest of your life.

—George Carlin